Making the Connections A collection of community stories from Pittsburgh'

Written by Justin Hopper   \   Edited by Dustin Stiver, Ryan Coon, and Matt Hannigan

The Pittsburgh 250 Community Connections Projects: 100 compelling initiatives that engaged citizens, addressed pressing issues, left a lasting impact on communities, and contributed to the "Pride & Progress" of Southwestern Pennsylvania in 2008. Led by established and emerging civic leaders, they created a critical mass of grassroots activity throughout the anniversary year.

More than 500 funding requests were received and decisions were made by regional and local panels representative of all 14 counties of Southwestern Pennsylvania. Most Regional Projects received awards of $50,000 to catalyze their efforts, while most Grassroots Projects received $5,000.

With projects, events, and activities happening in every county, residents of Southwestern Pennsylvania made history of their own during this watershed year — re-engaging neighbors, restoring connections, reinvigorating communities, and imagining what they can do here.

Nº 75\100 Indiana County Covered Bridge Festival Awarded: $5,000

Downtown Pittsburgh

A Letter from the Chairman of Pittsburgh 250:
A Regional Perspective

It's been 250 years since Pittsburgh's founding fathers imagined a new future here in Southwestern Pennsylvania, christening the town and setting in motion the events that would lead to the Pittsburgh region that we know today. Since then, this region has enjoyed a richness of history and a diversity of populations and experiences rarely matched by its neighboring American cities.

With Pittsburgh 250, we have celebrated that past and looked to the region's future with events and projects both large and small—from the nationally regarded Tour of Pennsylvania race and PNC Legacy Trail Ride, to homecomings and community gatherings of all shapes and sizes. As a major component of that commemoration, Community Connections helped 100 projects across the 14-county region to create their own ways to illuminate their past and imagine their future anew, bringing Pittsburgh 250 the broadest base of participation possible.

Pittsburgh 250's theme—Imagine What You Can Do Here—is about connecting the people inside and outside of this region to the vast wealth of ideas, amenities, and possibilities that Pittsburgh prizes as its greatest resources. As you'll see in the following pages, Community Connections helped accomplish that goal in a broad range of meaningful ways, across an impressive geographic area.

I'd like to thank the hundreds of people who took part in Community Connections for helping to make Pittsburgh 250 as great a success as it was, and to encourage them to take those new ideas and connections forward into Pittsburgh's next 250 years. *Making the Connections* is the story of a region and its citizens, and how they came together to celebrate their joint history by propelling their communities forward. I hope it helps you to think about the Pittsburgh region in a new light, and to imagine what you too can do here.

JAMES E. ROHR
Chairman, Pittsburgh 250th Anniversary Commission
Chairman and CEO, The PNC Financial Services Group

A Letter from the Community Connections Committee Co-Chairs:
Observations on Creativity, Collaboration

In late 2005, the Allegheny Conference on Community Development called us together to discuss a budding concept. We were asked to develop the community component of Pittsburgh 250. A mission with few parameters, but three ambitious goals: grassroots inclusivity, regional collaboration, and new models of community engagement.

Over the course of the next three years, with the help of hundreds of people from around the region, our initial ideas solidified into an initiative that has involved thousands more, created a new model for community-based philanthropic work, and built new networks that will continue to help the region grow for years to come. Through this work, we've seen communities both small and large draw closer together, and a renewed sense of understanding between the city and the countryside. We've seen how the potential for progress only increases as our discussions become more collaborative, our missions more inclusive, and our vision more expansive. Most importantly, we've seen a common recognition, among people involved at all levels of this process, that community connections are important, powerful, and precious things.

Many people from around Southwestern Pennsylvania deserve credit for further developing the program, and enabling Community Connections to exceed our initial goals. The more than 40 regional leaders who came together as the Community Connections Committee were integral in streamlining and acting upon the initiative's plans. Community Connections wouldn't have made it past the idea stage without the leadership and stewardship of the region's generous foundation community. Likewise, without the financial support and relationship-building power of the area's community foundations and corporate funders, Community Connections couldn't have encompassed the range it did. Moreover, The Sprout Fund's continued work in all corners of the region is at the heart of everything that Community Connections has accomplished.

But such credit is largely academic compared to that deserved by the hundreds of community leaders, project managers, decision-makers, and participants across the 14-county region. Their creativity, time, and bottomless wells of energy are the source of the 100 projects that will become the lasting legacy of Community Connections. It has been our absolute privilege to be a part of your work, and to watch Pittsburgh 250 connect county to county, neighbor to neighbor, and the past to the present in building our region's future.

ARADHNA M. DHANDA
President and CEO
Leadership Pittsburgh, Inc.

CATHY LEWIS LONG
Founding Executive Director
The Sprout Fund

GEORGE L. MILES JR.
President and CEO
WQED Multimedia

Trail Town Public Art Project, Westmoreland County

PITTSBURGH 250 COMMUNITY CONNECTIONS WAS SUPPORTED BY A DIVERSE ARRAY OF PRIVATE FOUNDATIONS, CORPORATIONS, AND COMMUNITY FOUNDATIONS FROM ACROSS SOUTHWESTERN PENNSYLVANIA.

Corporations

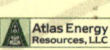

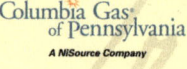

Private Foundations

Claude Worthington Benedum Foundation

The Grable Foundation

Hillman Foundation

Jewish Healthcare Foundation

Laurel Foundation

Richard King Mellon Foundation

Donald & Sylvia Robinson Family Foundation

Media Partners

deepLocal

Pittsburgh *Post-Gazette*

WDUQ 90.5 FM

Community Foundations

Armstrong County Community Foundation

Community Foundation for the Alleghenies

The Community Foundation of Fayette County

The Community Foundation of Greene County

Community Foundation of Western Pennsylvania and Eastern Ohio

The Community Foundation of Westmoreland County

The Pittsburgh Foundation

    Elmer G. and Gladys Schade Klaber Fund

    The Clarence G. Koepke Memorial Fund

    Ray H. Kohl Fund

    Phillip M. LeMaistre Fund

    Fannie A. Lawrence Fund

    The Lois Tack Thompson Fund

    William Christopher and Mary Laughlin Robinson Fund

PITTSBURGH AT 250: A PREFACE

The story of Pittsburgh's founding has all the elements one could ask of a great American legend. A martyr, in the defeat and death of General Edward Braddock as he marched on the French at the forks of the Ohio River. General John Forbes is its redeemer, his men laboriously cutting a trail through the wilderness from Philadelphia to attack Fort Duquesne—this time, successfully. George Washington completes the pantheon, standing with Forbes in November of 1758, at the place where three rivers meet to claim the surrounding land in the name of British statesman William Pitt.

When it came time, 250 years later, to mark that anniversary, it was obvious to the Pittsburgh 250 Commission and the Allegheny Conference on Community Development—the organization entrusted with coordinating events and activities related to the anniversary—that the date required a celebration that mirrored the iconic history of the Pittsburgh region.

At the Point—the historic site of Fort Duquesne—a $35 million renovation upgraded the State Park at Pittsburgh's heart. The Tour of Pennsylvania bicycle race attracted elite young cyclists from around the world to ride in a Philadelphia-to-Pittsburgh competition retracing the Forbes Trail, and nearly 100 other cyclists joined in the 335-mile ride celebrating the opening of the Great Allegheny Passage Washington, D.C.-to-Pittsburgh trail. Many homecomings and reunions brought 50,000 visitors back to Pittsburgh throughout 2008, many of whom were able to see world-class art exhibits and performances thanks to the Pittsburgh International Festival of Firsts and the Carnegie International.

Pittsburgh 250 also recognized some of Pittsburgh's most notable native sons and daughters, who were fêted at the History Makers Gala. Among the honored guests recognized for their impact on the region were historian and biographer David McCullough, actress Shirley Jones, philanthropist Teresa Heinz, and football great Franco Harris.

To the outside world, Pittsburgh may be most well known for the moments when its legends made history, be that Andrew Carnegie's revolution in steelmaking, the many National Football Championships of the Pittsburgh Steelers, or Jonas Salk stepping out of his University of Pittsburgh lab with the world's polio vaccine.

However, Pittsburgh's story is not only "the biography of great men," nor is it a mere timeline of pivotal events confined to the city's limits. It is a chronicle of incremental shifts and exceptional but unassuming individuals; one that takes place as much in a schoolroom or a neighborhood club as in a boardroom or science lab. It's the stories that occurred in Bedford and Butler counties where Forbes and Washington camped, and in the pioneer towns of Greene County where settlers launched a new nation's Westward expansion.

Pittsburgh's biography is Gus Greenlee in his Crawford Grill in the Hill District, grooming a generation of jazz players who would create "America's classical music." It's Wilma Scott Heide growing up in Connellsville, imagining a world where women are treated *as equals*. And it's the communities of Cambria County and the Mon Valley, producing the coal and the steel that built the American century.

In the same way, the 250th anniversary had to include momentous events and stories of legendary figures, just like the region had produced momentous history and legendary personalities. But it also had to include recognition of those individuals who keep the region's wheels constantly in motion, even when no mark appears on the timeline.

When we look back at the founding of Pittsburgh in the fall of 1758, we don't see a single day on which this place came to be—nor is our vision for this region's next 250 years so firmly cast. Rather, ours is an evolving story of people and events, both grand and small, covering hundreds of miles and including millions of voices.

Tour of Pennsylvania bicycle race, Hot Metal Bridge, Pittsburgh

01: FORGING CIVIC INNOVATION

When Pittsburgh celebrated its 200th anniversary in 1958, the "Pittsburgh Renaissance" of Mayor David L. Lawrence was well underway. Using its bicentennial as a moment to chart a new course, the city looked to a future without the soot and smog that it was famous for—a chance, under the slogan of "Gateway to the Future," to quite literally clear the air. At the time, the region's leadership envisioned a future built as much around banking, education, and technology as the past was built around the steel mills along the rivers.

CALL AND RESPONSE

So when it came time to celebrate the 250th anniversary in 2008, the Pittsburgh 250 Commission was faced with a challenge. With Pittsburgh's "smoky old town" image finally on its way out, and the transition to a more diverse and global economy underway, how could Pittsburgh best capitalize on this moment? In a time when regions now rise and fall together as collections of cooperative and interdependent communities rather than isolated and stratified rivals, the Commission recognized that the best possible future for Southwestern Pennsylvania is one in which everyone—from the smallest boroughs of the most distant counties to the largest corporations in the tallest skyscrapers—has a stake in the place they call home.

Searching for inspiration, the Commission looked to Jamestown, Virginia, where the historic colonial town celebrated its 400th anniversary in 2007 by connecting small community events and projects to the larger-scale anniversary events. With this kind of collaborative spirit in mind, the Commission approached three leaders of dynamic, nonprofit organizations to adapt this model to suit the Pittsburgh region at this moment in time.

"The challenge was how to be truly inclusive," says Aradhna Dhanda, president and CEO of Leadership Pittsburgh. "We wanted to learn from the people throughout this process, and then help them find ways they could celebrate the region's anniversary."

The trio of Dhanda, George Miles, Jr., president and CEO of WQED Multimedia, and Cathy Lewis Long, founding executive director of The Sprout Fund, became the co-chairs of the Community Connections Committee.

"This entire project had to come from the bottom up," says George Miles, "it had to come from the people. There's a lot of talk about 'regionalism'—we really wanted that. We wanted folks in Greene County or in Greensburg to feel as much a part of this as those in the middle of Pittsburgh."

The co-chairs, together with their committee of more than 40 leaders from Southwestern Pennsylvania, quickly realized that the answer was for Community Connections not to rebrand existing community projects under the banner of a larger initiative, but to cultivate and support new ideas created by and important to the region's people. The program would draw resources from a wide selection of regional community foundations, private foundations, and corporate donors to create a pool of funds that could then be used to make small grants to organizations and individuals seeking to engage and empower communities during the commemorative celebration.

Bill Flanagan asks: How do you make a city's anniversary something an entire region can celebrate?

It's a question that three partners set out to answer in 2004, when they came together at the request of Allegheny County Executive Dan Onorato and then City of Pittsburgh Mayor Tom Murphy. The Allegheny Conference on Community Development, the Heinz History Center and VisitPittsburgh developed a strategic blueprint for Pittsburgh 250 and organized the Pittsburgh 250th Anniversary Commission.

We knew there would be permanent improvements and major community events. We commemorated the Forbes Trail across Pennsylvania and supported the completion of the Great Allegheny Passage—a 300-mile biking and hiking trail from Washington, D.C. to Pittsburgh—as well as the transformation of Point State Park. We showcased the projects with events covering 300 miles, an international bike race from Philadelphia, a community trail ride from Washington, D.C., and a two-month Festival of Lights. We promoted numerous arts and cultural premieres, from the Carnegie Museums and the Pittsburgh Cultural Trust to the Frick Art & Historical Center and the Heinz History Center. Hundreds of thousands of people turned out and millions more learned about it in media coverage worldwide.

But the almost 200 members of the Commission were determined not to limit the celebrations to the City of Pittsburgh's anniversary. They wanted to make Pittsburgh 250 as regional as possible in scope. The reason was simple: In today's global economy, winning the competition for tourists, talented workers, and investment depends upon everything an entire region has to offer.

It helped that two other major 250th anniversary celebrations were already being planned in Bedford and in Ligonier, Westmoreland County. Both were named during the Forbes Campaign of 1758 that also led to the naming of Pittsburgh. Partnering with them was straightforward. The challenge was to find a way to include communities in 11 other counties in Southwestern Pennsylvania. And that was the genesis of Community Connections.

We borrowed the name of the initiative from Jamestown 400 and turned it over to the Community Connections Committee and later to The Sprout Fund with a promise to help raise one million dollars. Why a million? Because even today, people tend to pay attention if you say you're going to give away "a million bucks."

Oh, and we had one other requirement: The process to select the community projects funded by the initiative had to be as grassroots as possible. We didn't want there to be any perception that "Pittsburgh" was playing favorites or picking winners.

So, here we are, five years later, summing up a truly remarkable record of grassroots decisionmaking and community outreach. I think it's safe to say that Community Connections and The Sprout Fund far exceeded our expectations by inventing a whole new way to connect and galvanize communities across our region.

We hope as a result of Community Connections that people throughout the 14 counties have a better sense of the heritage we all share and a renewed pride in where we are today. Most of all, we hope that they will be ready and willing to work together again to make "Greater Pittsburgh" even greater in the future.

BILL FLANAGAN
Executive Director,
Pittsburgh 250

At first, it sounds like a straightforward idea: Give people money to invest in their own communities. But to ensure the money was awarded to the projects most valuable to participating communities, the Community Connections Committee flipped the standard model of philanthropy on its side.

It wasn't just a new model that was required, but a whole new paradigm. While regional planning bodies have long developed high-level plans for the multi-county region, there was no system for organizing the hundreds of community organizations, service agencies, and engaged individuals at work in the region. Community Connections would give communities the power to decide for themselves where and how the region's philanthropic dollars would be awarded.

The Committee realized that an initiative this large and bold couldn't be operated by volunteers alone. This kind of work was cut out for an organization experienced in many of the facets that the initiative would require—and one already invested in creating the Community Connections concept.

Since its inception in 2001, The Sprout Fund had worked in the Pittsburgh area, funding and managing small projects through a variety of programs.

Sprout had made its name by catalyzing civic innovation, supporting unorthodox approaches to complex problems, and engaging communities to enact creative solutions to a variety of challenges. Programs like its signature Seed Award program, which makes small-scale funding awards to dozens of new projects each year, and its Public Art program, which leverages collaboration between local artists and community members to galvanize grassroots participation and decisionmaking, positioned Sprout as an organization with community decision-making experience that stood between the "treetops" and the grassroots.

And for Sprout, building the Community Connections process wouldn't have to be done from scratch. As Board Chair Henry Simonds points out, it was more a matter of summing up Sprout's proven strengths.

"We were able to incorporate elements from the Seed Award program, the Public Art program, and experience bringing large groups to the table with initiatives like Engage Pittsburgh and the Idea Round-Up," says Simonds. "Taken in isolation, those programs are all great, but also disparate. For Community Connections, we put them all together to create something that's sum was greater than the whole of its parts."

FUNDRAISING CHANGE

Community Connections set an ambitious fundraising goal of one million dollars to support projects in each of the 14 counties of Southwestern Pennsylvania. To plant new seeds, significant investment had to be made not just in Pittsburgh or Allegheny County, but in neighboring counties, towns and villages; communities that are of equal importance to the region's history and future prosperity.

Fundraising was an integral part of the process of connecting communities—whether that was a small community foundation an hour's drive south of Pittsburgh, or the corporate giving office of the region's nationally known banks. As president of the Claude Worthington Benedum Foundation, the first private foundation to give to Community Connections, Pat Getty knows as well as anyone that raising money is about more than filling the pot. It's the way that the philanthropic community builds its own connections.

"Funding is a part of the problem with a top-down structure," says Getty. "We have to recognize that we need a more horizontal approach to every aspect of community life—an approach that engages a variety of people and organizations by inclusion. So it was important to get as many funders as possible for Community Connections."

Sprout's Cathy Lewis Long points out that this kind of fundraising outreach was part of Community Connections' model from the very start.

"It was incumbent upon us to have a base of support that reflected the initiative's inclusiveness," says Lewis Long. "We knew that we wouldn't be able to raise significant dollars in the outlying counties. But we also knew that we needed strong partners in each county, and community foundations are the ones working in those communities."

It wasn't until its sixth birthday, in 2007, that the Community Foundation of Greene County made its first regular, annual discretionary grants—the first regular assets, in other words, that the community foundation awarded other than pre-determined gifts. Rather than a project based in its county seat of Waynesburg, or one of the small but vibrant cultural organizations in Greensboro, that year the foundation made a $1,000 grant to Community Connections. And according to Executive Director Bettie Stammerjohn, it was a decision that was both easy to make, and important for the sparsely populated rural county.

"Until 1990, the population was small enough that we weren't even counted in the Southwestern Pennsylvania regional census information," says Stammerjohn. "Greene County was really overlooked for a long time. So we place a priority on helping to build the place of Greene County within the region. We saw the benefit of encouraging Sprout and Community Connections to be here—it benefits the county just to be a part of this regional initiative."

Along with seven community foundations, Community Connections received funding from six private foundations such as Benedum and the Richard King Mellon Foundation, and eight corporate funders. According to Leslie Orbin, manager of communications and community relations for Columbia Gas of Pennsylvania, a NiSource Company, the project was ideal for their giving plans, and those of other regional companies.

"We were interested in being involved in Pittsburgh 250, because of the company's rich history in Southwestern Pennsylvania," says Orbin. "For companies that work in all 14 counties in the region, a program that would impact small organizations in those counties was something we wanted to be a part of."

Just as Community Connections would give the grassroots a stake in Pittsburgh 250 through small-scale Grassroots Projects, the initiative would make several larger funding awards to Regional Projects that affected many communities in multiple counties.

Ideation sketch

"Something Community Connections did," says Benedum's Getty, "was to demonstrate that there's enthusiasm about working across the region towards change. That's not something that happens without some kind of a nudge to broker connections throughout the region's philanthropic community."

IDEA FARMING

Similar to its approach to fundraising, finding the projects and community leaders that would ultimately be funded by Community Connections called for a more considered approach than issuing a generic call for proposals. Through a series of idea generation, or "ideation," sessions held in every county in the region, The Sprout Fund helped catalyze and foster ideas that would celebrate the "Pride and Progress" of this region— the theme of Community Connections—whether that was through an established organization, or just a few hard-working folks with a great idea.

To Valerie Huston, who attended the Armstrong County session, the issue concerning her seemed like a fairly simple fact of life: Food does not originate in the supermarket. Before it can be packaged and marketed, presented and paid for, food has to be grown by men and women working on farms like the one she lived on. But to so many American schoolchildren—even kids growing up in rural Western Pennsylvania— this basic fact is beyond their ken. "Ask an elementary school student where eggs come from, they say, 'Foodland,'" says Tonya Wible, program manager of Pennsylvania's Mobile Agriculture-Education (Ag/Ed) Science Lab. "Even in rural areas, they're losing that connection with agriculture."

One solution to this problem is a fleet of Pennsylvania Farm Bureau-operated mobile agricultural science labs that are able to pull up outside schools and give students hands-on learning experiences. But when Valerie Huston heard about the program in 2007, it was largely limited to the Eastern and Central parts of the state. Huston thought it was about time Western Pennsylvania had a dedicated lab of its own. She met with potential supporters such as the Armstrong County Commissioner's office and Armstrong Educational Trust, who suggested she attend a workshop led by The Sprout Fund's Community Connections Program Coordinator Dustin Stiver. And it was there that she discovered that community projects don't just come from the big organizations—sometimes they, too, have to start 'on the farm.'

"I gave a presentation on my project, and Dustin said, 'I think I've heard this idea before.' He put me in touch with Henry Karki, who he had met at the Mercer County ideation session and was working on the same project with the Beaver-Lawrence Farm Bureau, and we wrote the grant together." After surviving multiple rounds of review, the Mobile Ag/Ed Science Lab project successfully navigated the decisionmaking process to receive a $50,000 Regional Grant. The new lab debuted in July, 2008, to a fully booked schedule visiting schools around the region.

"Many of the applications we received following the ideation sessions were from individuals that had never engaged in this type of activity before," says Stiver. "Our goal was to reach into communities by designing a program that solicited ideas from both professional grantwriters and everyday citizens alike, and I think we accomplished that. Hundreds of people showed up, some with long-held ambitions, and others with freshly hatched ideas, but all demonstrating a passion for their community."

At the sessions, held in each of the 14 counties of Southwestern Pennsylvania, a moderator led group discussions that encouraged participants to think of creative solutions to meet the needs of their communities. Afterwards, the most promising concepts were discussed further in breakout groups, to see what kinds of proposals for Community Connections grants might come forth.

N°: 07\100   **Mobile Ag/Ed Science Lab**   Awarded: $50,000

It might be better known for steel and industry, but Southwestern Pennsylvania has always been a region built on its farmlands— and agriculture remains an important facet of the region's economy. Which makes it especially disconcerting when the region's children, asked a question such as "Where does corn come from?" often answer "the supermarket." Inside the refitted RV that houses Western Pennsylvania's Mobile Ag/Ed Science Lab, students learn that agriculture is more than just farmland they pass on the road. During the Lab's multi-day sessions at regional schools, kids participate in exercises such as "A Day in Your Life with Agriculture," learning that everything from their cotton clothes to the pizza they had for lunch has its roots in the soil and the people who work it.

Mike Kane asks:
How do you
build solid
foundations?

Community foundations exist to connect donors to issues and opportunities in the communities they serve. Often, community foundations help identify local concerns; at other times we act in support of efforts that meet common goals. In the largest sense, community foundations provide support, initiate discussions and the exchange of ideas, and spur change as needed.

Sounds an awful lot like the goals of Pittsburgh 250, doesn't it?

That's why the Community Foundation for the Alleghenies and our colleagues were so enthused about participating in Pittsburgh 250 Community Connections. In all, seven community foundations, with geographic areas of interest covering most of the Southwestern Pennsylvania region, stepped up to help fund the effort. The money we provided helped in a modest way to round out the funding for the events and projects supported by Community Connections.

Speaking for our foundation, I'm certainly glad we did it. But our financial contribution was by no means the extent of our participation. What mattered more was the work I like to think community foundations do best: We connected the goals and energy of Pittsburgh 250 with the people and communities of our region. And, in return, we connected those same people to a larger idea—one that needed them to be successful in a regional approach.

It's common to assume everyone knows what everyone else is up to in some more rural counties, but of course, that's not always the case. After funding was secured, a team of moderators and graphic facilitators hit the road to raise awareness and gather ideas for the upcoming funding opportunity. Community foundations were essential to this process as we helped schedule meetings and get the word out in our territory. I attended the Somerset County session and was impressed with the ideas and the sense of possibility as people fed off each other's creativity. They were there in hopes of having their projects funded, of course, but that didn't seem to me to be the only reason for all the excitement in the room. What Community Connections brought was a chance to be heard—for people to talk about what they valued and why they value it.

Certainly, encouraging those in our region to be a part of something larger is what community foundations, and Community Connections, are all about.

One project funded in Cambria County replaced a former small junkyard with native planting and a multi-leveled gateway landscape. The leader for the community group told me she was surprised the effort was funded because she didn't imagine her project was big enough to warrant the attention. She and her group have since taken on another garden, and now she's thinking of running for city council.

And that's just one of many stories that confirms the important role that Community Connections has played in reengaging people—giving them the tools, resources, and most importantly, the inspiration to take a greater hand in the life of their communities. Whether I look at it as a Community Connections participant, a community foundation representative, or just as a member of my community, I call that success.

MIKE KANE

Executive Director,
Community Foundations
for the Alleghenies

Brainstorming notes, Somerset County

Ideation session, Greene County

According to Katrina Struloeff, marketing and development coordinator at the Union Project, a Pittsburgh-based nonprofit community center, and an ideation session moderator, the moderator's job was part traffic cop—making sure everyone had their chance to speak—and part detective—investigating and probing ideas put forth by participants.

"We were empowering people to recognize that their ideas could be something," says Struloeff, and to draw from the participants the true worth of their projects. "We were there to ask, 'How would you explain the importance of your idea to someone who has never been to Cambria County before?'"

As attendees talked, several graphic facilitators—artists drafted from the Pittsburgh area—drew their impressions of each project, to create a visual complement to the verbal discussion. Pittsburgh illustrator Chris Schmidt served as graphic facilitator for several sessions. To him, the graphic facilitator's job wasn't just to draw peoples' ideas, but to show the group what they had in common.

"People who develop collective ideas, they're like the blind men trying to describe the elephant," says Schmidt. "Each understands a part of it—but what does it all look like? When you finally detail that, visually, you generally find there's consensus."

Even in smaller areas, the widespread call for ideas brought new faces into the grantmaking process—people who might have never considered applying for a grant, or even beginning a project, in other circumstances.

When Dr. Stephen Catt, executive director of planning and external relations at Butler County Community College, co-hosted his county's ideation session, he saw something come out of the meeting besides a handful of potential Community Connections project ideas.

"The money was the lure that brought everybody together," says Catt, but perhaps not the most important part of the ideation sessions. "People gravitate towards their own networks, and once you're in your own world, it's hard to break out. The best part of these sessions were the new communications—the new networks that came out of them."

GRANTING WISHES

Community Connections was created and funded through regional collaboration. But none of those efforts would have been very meaningful without a similarly democratic process for deciding which projects to fund.

"It was essential for the decisionmaking process to create opportunities for local perspectives," says The Sprout Fund's Lewis Long. "For example, Somerset County representatives needed to consider Somerset County applications. And, in the same way, Regional applications needed to be reviewed through a regional lens."

IT WAS ESSENTIAL THAT THE DECISIONMAKING PROCESS CREATE OPPORTUNITIES FOR LOCAL PERSPECTIVES.

Allegheny County decisionmaking meeting

When it came time to create that decisionmaking process, however, Sprout was faced with a problem—albeit a good one: Community Connections had garnered 522 project applications, far more than had been expected. On September 14, 2007, the submission deadline, Sprout received an application every six minutes. They came in from across the spectrum of Southwestern Pennsylvania—both geographically, and in terms of project focus, with applicants ranging from churches and community organizations to museums, schools, and even farmers. One memorable application delivery—from Family Communications, Inc.—was an especially speedy delivery via *Mister Rogers' Neighborhood* star Mr. McFeely.

Grassroots project applications—those requesting $5,000 or less for projects affecting a single community or county—were reviewed by panels of decisionmakers chosen from within each county, reflective of that county's demographic makeup and nominated by county residents. Each decisionmaker rated project proposals based on criteria developed by The Sprout Fund, including anticipated impact on the community and intended audience; contributions to goals such as connecting communities and civic engagement; and of course, feasibility for success. Then, at decisionmaking forums, those applications were discussed and the funding decisions made by the panel members.

"A lot of the projects we reviewed, I'd never even heard of them," says Michael Wright, executive director of Shenango Valley Urban League and a Grassroots decisionmaker for Mercer County. "And these were people right here in my backyard. It provided a whole new avenue for smaller or minority-run projects to find funding."

By recruiting dozens of people like Wright, Community Connections helped ensure that Grassroots funding decisions were based on the specific needs and priorities of each county. With decisionmakers ranging from philanthropists to business people, state representatives to borough officials, academics and community organizers, the unique make-up of Southwestern Pennsylvania's 14 counties was reflected in the constitution of the Grassroots decisionmaking panels.

All told, 88 Grassroots Projects received support totaling $418,750. Although, with more than 230 applications vying for Regional Grants requesting up to $50,000 each, that decisionmaking process was even more rigorous.

To ensure that only the strongest candidates would be considered by decisionmakers, experts from a variety of fields reviewed Regional applications. In total, 75 expert reviewers from fields as diverse as education and agriculture, government and environmentalism, were brought in to help identify the projects with the highest potential for success. One of those reviewers, looking in particular at neighborhood development projects, was Wanda Wilson.

"I reviewed quite a few projects falling into two categories," says Wilson, a program officer at the Pittsburgh Partnership for Neighborhood Development. "There was a cluster of projects that wanted to work on neighborhood improvement projects, and another cluster of projects that wanted to document the history of a community."

"I evaluated projects against the criteria Sprout provided, which really led me to consider projects that would have an impact on the specific community and also meet broader goals," says Wilson.

Once proposals were examined and rated by the expert reviewers, The Sprout Fund provided the top tier of proposals to the Regional Decisionmaking Panel. For the applicants who made it through this round of examination, there was one more step they had to take on their approach to receiving support.

At the Regional Decisionmaking Forum held in Pittsburgh on December 13, 2007, the 24 strongest Regional Grant candidates presented their ideas live before the decisionmakers from all counties. After each project was given a chance to make their case to the assembled body of decisionmakers, deliberations ensued and, after an exhaustive dialogue, 12 Regional projects were chosen to receive grants of up to $50,000.

JoAnn McBride, executive director of the Lawrence County Tourist Promotion Agency, served as one of the decisionmakers on the Regional panel. Through this experience, she felt she was able to make a positive impact not just for Lawrence County, but to keep in sight Community Connections' goal of being truly regional.

"I thought all the projects we chose were really strong," says McBride. "The rural communities around Pittsburgh are in constant contact, and we're used to making compromises with Pittsburgh. Sometimes it feels like Pittsburgh muscles its way through, but not here. In this process, every county got something—it was a big regional effort, and I felt honored to be there."

At the Regional decisionmaking forum, Fellows from the Coro Center for Civic Leadership in Pittsburgh mediated round-table discussions. To mediator and Coro alumna Sujata Shyam, the method was not only successful as a decision-making system, but also in revealing the extent of the region's commitment to community progress.

"The process was amazing to see," says Shyam, "the presentations by finalists, the round-table discussions, and the final large group discussion. It was an impressive operation to bring this group to consensus. I'd recently moved to Pittsburgh from San Francisco, and I was inspired by the projects that made it to the regional forum. It offered a fantastic perspective on civic engagement in this region."

Diasmer Bloe, Allegheny County Decisionmaker

As senior producer at WQED-TV, Minnette Seate is no stranger to the world of nonprofit community programming. But Seate possesses another trait that made her perfect to act as a member of the Regional decisionmaking panel: She's no sucker for jargon.

"I suppose I should call it 'perspective,' but I brought a lot of my own 'baggage' to the decisionmaking table," says Seate. "I tried to be as even-handed as possible—but with a heaping teaspoon of reality."

Yet by the end of the process, Seate had discovered another important aspect of the decisionmaking system. She saw dozens of individuals from around the region display ingenuity and passion for bettering their communities. And it brought her a new perspective on the region—one that left her "baggage" behind, and connected her more closely to the presenters, her fellow decisionmakers, and the places from which they all come.

"It opened my eyes to how Pittsburgh-centric I can be," says Seate. "You forget sometimes that while others may vote or dress a bit differently than you, they want the same basic things for their communities that I do—just with a different dressing on it."

AWARDS AND ALLIES

On the morning of December 19, 2007, more than 300 people gathered at the top of the Regional Enterprise Tower in Downtown Pittsburgh. At first glance, the attendees may not have seemed to have much in common. This disparate group included Pittsburgh business leaders in two-button suits and historical reenactors in 18th-century military uniforms; philanthropy professionals from the region's south in Greene County and farmers from its north in Armstrong; community organizers from Homewood and Girl Scout leaders from Mercer County.

But as many of them learned that day, they certainly did have a lot in common. They had a firm belief in the potential of Southwestern Pennsylvania, and a bright idea of how to build a better future while celebrating the past as a part of Pittsburgh 250. What's more, each had something in common—whether they were cleaning up a small community in Cambria County or building huge sculptures throughout the region: A Community Connections check had their name on it.

Once those checks were handed out, and the Regional Enterprise Tower cleared of guests, those projects shared something else: A year-long relationship with The Sprout Fund, which proceeded to act as sounding board, advocate, PR firm and general assistant to all 100 projects funded through Community Connections. If one of the important facets of Community Connections was its ability to empower new and inexperienced grassroots community activists by funding their projects, it would've been a grave mistake not to back up that funding with other kinds of support throughout the year.

As Sprout's Community Connections Program Coordinator, Dustin Stiver found himself hitting the highways and byways of Southwestern Pennsylvania throughout 2008 in aid of the initiative's projects.

"We knew from the outset that distributing checks was only the beginning of our work," says Stiver. "Sprout has experience helping new projects move from 'requests to results.' It was important to work alongside project managers to equip them for success."

Sometimes it was enough just to support a project by showing up, say, at the unveiling of a new beautification effort in Ambridge. Other times, that support role became more complex—advocating for the South Side Sculpture Project at public forums, or creating and issuing press releases and media requests for event-driven projects. Still others required something else entirely, such as when the Parker Postage Stamp Park called with a beguiling question: "What actually *happens* at a groundbreaking ceremony?"

Perhaps most importantly, Sprout was there—at the other end of the phone, out in the field, and through a monthly online newsletter—to keep reminding projects that they're not alone. Through Community Connections, Sprout helped build a new regional network of committed partners, including community groups, funding organizations, media outlets, and just regular folks willing to turn out and put in a few hours. Throughout 2008, the region would see this new network of Community Connections come alive to empower the people of Southwestern Pennsylvania.

With grant money in pocket, the 100 projects funded through Community Connections got down to business balancing their limited funds with their lofty goals. But just as Sprout and the Community Connections Committee had hoped, when community members were given the opportunity to direct funding as they saw fit, supported projects rose to the occasion.

Though different in scope, divergent in goals, diverse in audience, and distant in geography, these projects together comprise the story of Pittsburgh 250 Community Connections.

02: ICONS

THERE'S SUCH A FANTASTIC TIMELESS QUALITY HERE, IT INSPIRED ME TO LEAVE SOMETHING PERMANENT FOR THE FUTURE—THESE COULD STILL BE HERE HUNDREDS OF YEARS FROM NOW.

Impressions. Expressions. Visions.

The creation and implementation of a work of public art can signal many things. It can be a step in a larger community effort, symbolizing pride in the neighborhood, or a commemoration of cultural and historical events that transpired therein. Sometimes the act of making the artwork itself is enough reason to proudly display its final product, created out of the raw talents and materials of the community.

Amongst the public art projects funded by Community Connections, certain artistic themes reappeared again and again: a permanence of concept and materials; pride of history in an act of forward progress; and, the contemplation of location and integration into community. But, perhaps most excitingly, none of these projects resulted in art unable or unwilling to stand the test of time. These icons will remain by the roads and trails of the region for years to come.

CAPTAINS OF INDUSTRY

Even in the bright sunshine of summer, entering the former LTV Steel coke-works along the Monongahela River near Pittsburgh's Hazelwood neighborhood can be somewhat intimidating. Past a cobwebbed guard's kiosk, one slowly drives down disused roads and into the mile-long building that once housed the works' rolling mill, where an iron giant, 20 feet tall, looms shadowy and watchful. This is zombie territory: the scorched earth and Frankenstein's monsters of the post-industrial age.

To acclaimed Pittsburgh artist Tim Kaulen, it's all raw material—from the scraps stacked in one corner of the mill, to the histories and myths that surround the city's industrial lore. With the other members of the Industrial Arts Co-Op, Kaulen has spent 10 years helping to forge the rusted detritus and proud iconography of Pittsburgh's industrial history into a monumental work—the South Side Sculpture Project. The sculpture is a multi-story-tall diorama of two steel workers built from pieces of the original nearby Hot Metal Bridge, framing an industrial crucible, its rim overrun with metal frozen in mid-pour.

The surroundings may seem intimidating initially, but it's obvious that Kaulen is as comfortable in the LTV site's massive studio space as in his living room. Arms crossed, ignoring the nearby welder's torches and nerve-rattling balanced girders, Kaulen shakes his head as his dog, Eli, runs around with a wooden spool, trying to lure a playmate. It ought to be comfortable after a decade's work.

"The Industrial Arts Co-op was commissioned for this by the City in 1998," as a central artwork for a new riverfront shopping area, says Kaulen. "It was meant for the Southside Works, which was in the planning stage."

At that time, the Southside Works was only an idea—a shopping and living development on the brownfield space that once housed the Jones & Laughlin steel mill. With the site's history in mind, the Co-op—a group of artists interested in large-scale public artwork—chose its subject matter and materials from that industrial heritage.

The group solicited a number of donations from the industry itself. Scrap metal from the LTV and Jones & Laughlin sites, salvaged from the recycling process, went to build the workers and their "armor," as Kaulen describes it: "A layer of metal, like protective gear. It's meant to get away from the architectural geometry of the figures—make them appear more organic." A Youngstown company donated a used hot-metal ladle—the ten-foot-tall, bucket-like iron piece that serves as the sculpture's centerpiece.

But the same things that make the sculpture compelling—it's larger-than-life scale, and time-weathered, permanent materials—created difficulties for the Co-op artists. Early into the process, it became clear that, while the city was interested in housing the piece at the Works, there was not a dedicated piece of land for it to reside on.

"There was never a specified site," says Kaulen, "but we decided to build it without the site, because we just wanted to make the art."

The LTV site in which the Co-op works, now owned by a consortium of foundations called the Almono Limited Partnership, is a godsend, according to Kaulen. It may be "freezing in winter, and too hot in summer," but its height and width makes the Co-op members uniquely able to work cheaply on the kinds of scale their work encompasses. The problem, however, has been in moving the piece, and reassembling it on its final South Side location. That's where the Regional Grant from Community Connections came in, providing money to finish work on the sculpture, and help transplant the multi-ton structure to its permanent home—and in doing so, create a new icon for future generations of Pittsburghers.

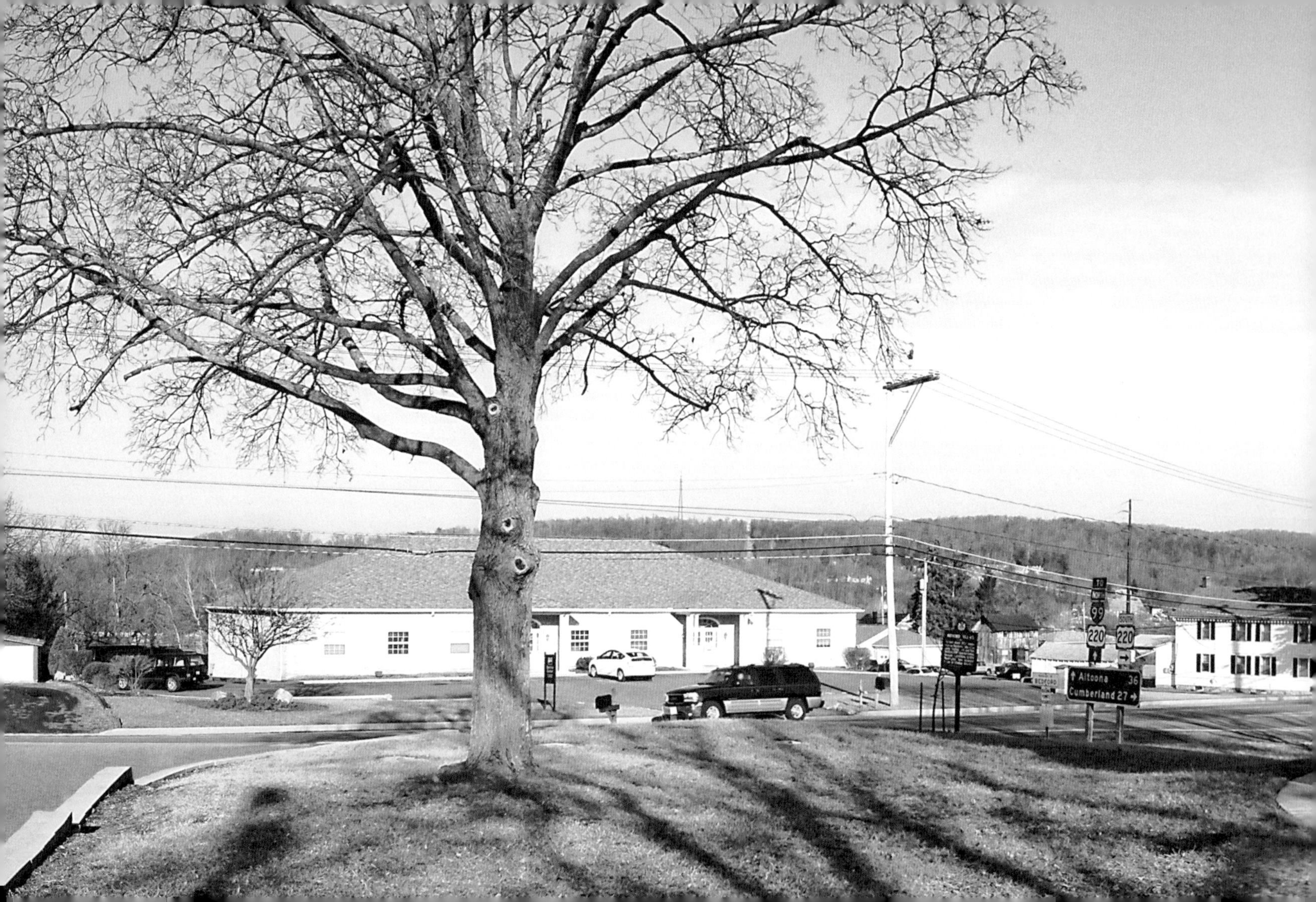
TO
99
220
220
Altoona 36
Cumberland 27

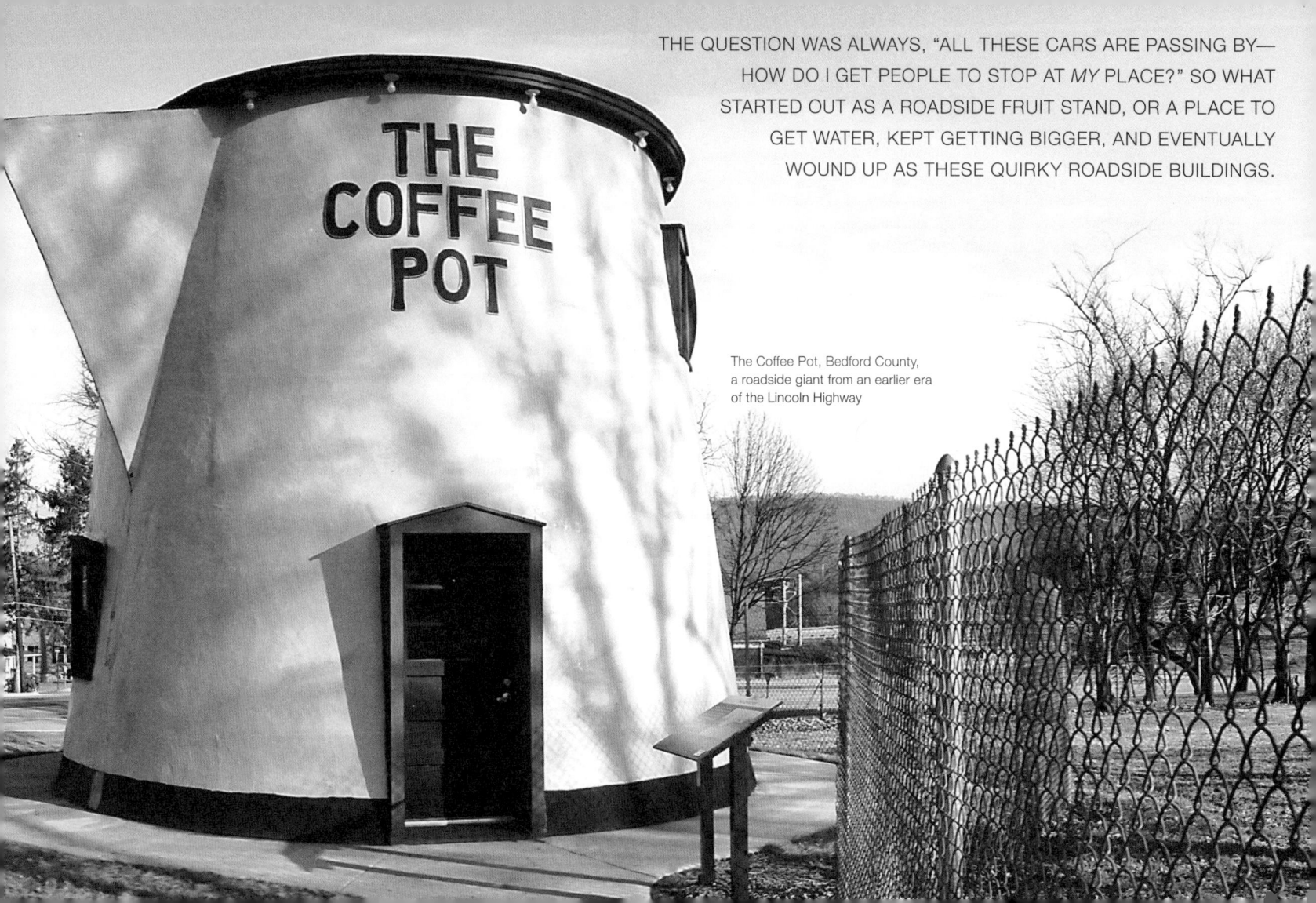

THE QUESTION WAS ALWAYS, "ALL THESE CARS ARE PASSING BY—HOW DO I GET PEOPLE TO STOP AT *MY* PLACE?" SO WHAT STARTED OUT AS A ROADSIDE FRUIT STAND, OR A PLACE TO GET WATER, KEPT GETTING BIGGER, AND EVENTUALLY WOUND UP AS THESE QUIRKY ROADSIDE BUILDINGS.

The Coffee Pot, Bedford County, a roadside giant from an earlier era of the Lincoln Highway

DRIVING AMBITIONS

Scale, permanence, histories of industry and a transitioning economy: When Olga Herbert talks about the public art project she's working on for the Lincoln Highway Heritage Corridor (LHHC), her language echoes that of the Industrial Arts Co-op. Not surprising, considering the geographic regions and historical eras that Herbert, as executive director of LHHC, deals with.

In its heyday, from 1913 until the opening of the Pennsylvania Turnpike in 1940, the Lincoln Highway was the primary East-West corridor through the state—part of a transcontinental road, Herbert is quick to point out, "ten years older than Route 66, and twice as long!" And unlike so much of Route 66, you can still get your kicks driving the entirety of the Lincoln Highway today from Times Square to San Francisco.

Pennsylvania's portion of the Highway is dotted by small towns that once brimmed with the roadside bustle that befit the country's prime thoroughfare, but which have fallen into economic and historical quietude since the coming of the Turnpike seven decades back. The LHHC exists, according to Herbert, to help promote economic development through tourism along the least populated portion of Pennsylvania's Lincoln Highway, from the Allegheny-Westmoreland County line to York County, over 200 miles away.

As part of that mission, the LHHC established the Roadside Giants of the Lincoln Highway project. With support from a Regional Grant, the LHHC partnered with four technical schools around the Western Pennsylvania region to create a series of Roadside Giants—huge, architectural structures in the form of commercial objects. It's a practice with a long history along the Lincoln Highway, the best-known example of which is Bedford County's Giant Coffee Pot.

"These people living along the Highway were real entrepreneurs," says Herbert. "The question was always, 'all these cars are passing by—how do I get people to stop at *my* place?' So what started out as a roadside fruit stand, or a place to get water, kept getting bigger and bigger, and eventually wound up being these quirky roadside buildings, often put up over the course of a weekend."

Students at the partnering schools designed and constructed a sculpture for their area's portion of the Highway. In doing so, the students gained valuable inter-disciplinary experience—the graphic design students handing concepts off to welders; the process moving on to the building-trade students, "who might say, 'there's not enough steel in the world to do this!'" It's a collaborative working environment that served to impart practical real-world knowledge to the participating students and enrich their learning experiences.

The finished pieces will each become iconographic for their locality: a Packard—the iconic car of the Lincoln Highway age—in Greensburg, Westmoreland County, created by Central Westmoreland Career and Technology Center in New Stanton, or a tandem bicycle in the town of Somerset—alluding to their many cycle trails—crafted by Somerset County Technology Center. But there's also a unifying aspect to the Roadside Giants. There'll be no missing these structures, and no doubting that you're riding on the age-old Lincoln Highway.

"Some people tend to disregard this kind of architecture," says Herbert, "but it's programmatic architecture: yeah, they stick out, that's what they're supposed to do."

Nº: **10**\100   **Roadside Giants of the Lincoln Highway**   Awarded: $49,340

It's a safe bet that, when these students matriculated into the Eastern Westmoreland Career and Technology Center, none of them envisioned the massive, multi-story gas pump sculpture that was in their educational future. But through Roadside Giants of the Lincoln Highway, not only have these Latrobe, Westmoreland County, students built such a thing, they've made it into a local icon: Along with colleagues from three other regional tech schools, Eastern student welders, designers, and even chefs (who baked celebratory cakes in the shape of each Giant), contributed to a new lasting legacy along this historic route.

LEADING TRAILERS

On the outskirts of Connellsville, in Fayette County, sit three 30-foot tall silos, each containing one of three substances used to make glass. When Chris Galiyas was asked to prime the silos for painting in 2008, he figured that'd be the beginning and end of his job. As a house painter, as well as a creative artist and West Mifflin art teacher, it's the kind of job Galiyas has done innumerous times. But standing on that scaffolding, day after day, Galiyas got to talking to the dozens of people he'd see hiking and biking on the Great Allegheny Passage, the 150-mile D.C.-to-Pittsburgh trail that winds near the silos.

"Prepping the silos, I saw hundreds of people going by each day on the Trail," says Galiyas. "I asked some people, 'what's it about' and 'how often do you use it,' and a few people each day would say they use it every day, 365 days per year. So I had this idea for the silos—about the four seasons, and how Connellsville changes. I submitted a drawing and a mock-up, and my idea got picked!"

Galiyas' painting—images of the seasons, rendered on a huge scale on the sides of the silos—is part of a chain of public artworks up and down the Great Allegheny Passage, at least one in each of the six Trail Towns on Western Pennsylvania's portion of that now-famous path. The Progress Fund, a Laurel Highlands economic development agency and the Trail Town Program's parent organization, received a Regional Grant to create new works of public art that express each town's vision for itself, using a strategy based on The Sprout Fund's Public Art program that matches communities with local artists to create permanent, collaborative works of art in public places.

The result was a broad range of artworks in an equal breadth of media: murals and sculptures in Confluence, Meyersdale and Rockwood in Somerset County; a sculpture made of railroad spikes in West Newton, Westmoreland County; and, in Fayette County, Connellsville's silos and trail-spanning arch, and three large etched stones in Ohiopyle. (Connellsville and Rockwood also received Grassroots Grants to further enhance their projects.)

Several of the pieces rely on themes of industrial legacy similar to those of the South Side Sculpture Project and Roadside Giants projects. Scott Hostettler's sculpture of a steam locomotive in Rockwood is one such example. Built out of metal and repurposed bicycle parts, Hostettler's sculpture literalizes the "rails-to-trails" concept behind the Great Allegheny Passage, reimagining the train sculpture as one built on the region's industrial past with hopes for a greener future.

Permanence also plays a role in these works. Laura DeFazio, a professor of art and design at California University of Pennsylvania, created Ohiopyle's Trail Town piece. DeFazio's work is decidedly permanent in nature: The pieces represent a thumbnail sketch of the biodiversity in Ohiopyle State Park, a naturalist haven. Divided into elemental categories: a dragonfly on the stone designated for Air creatures, rabbits for Earth, and a turtle for Water. Carved into the side of rough-hewn native sandstone, the pieces are akin to the petroglyphs DeFazio saw along the Cuyahoga while living in Ohio. And like those pieces, DeFazio says, these could stand for a long time.

"There's such a fantastic timeless quality about Ohiopyle," she says, "it inspired that sense of wanting to leave something permanent for the future—these could still be here hundreds of years from now."

It's a good example of the Trail Town goal—and, perhaps, that of all of these projects: to create public art that becomes intrinsically part of its location and remains an emblem of the community, even after the celebration of Pittsburgh 250 has long passed.

№ : 04\100   Great Allegheny Passage Trail Town Public Art Project   Awarded: $50,000

With their depiction of the four seasons, painted on the silos of the Youghiogheny Opalescent Glass Company in Connellsville, Fayette County, artists Chris Galiyas and Meeghan Triggs pay tribute to the year-round dedication of hikers and bikers along the Great Allegheny Passage that passes below. But it's not the only new icon that can be seen by travelers braving the journey from Washington, D.C. to Pittsburgh—the Trail Town Public Art Project created artwork all along the Pennsylvania portion of this 318 mile trail system. In Rockwood, Somerset County, sculptor Scott Hostettler fashioned a locomotive from reused materials and in Connellsville, Fayette County, sculptor Steven Fiscus erected an archway at the very spot where General Braddock's army crossed the river in 1755, and where those who would march to Pittsburgh today will find their ford, too.

[See following pages]

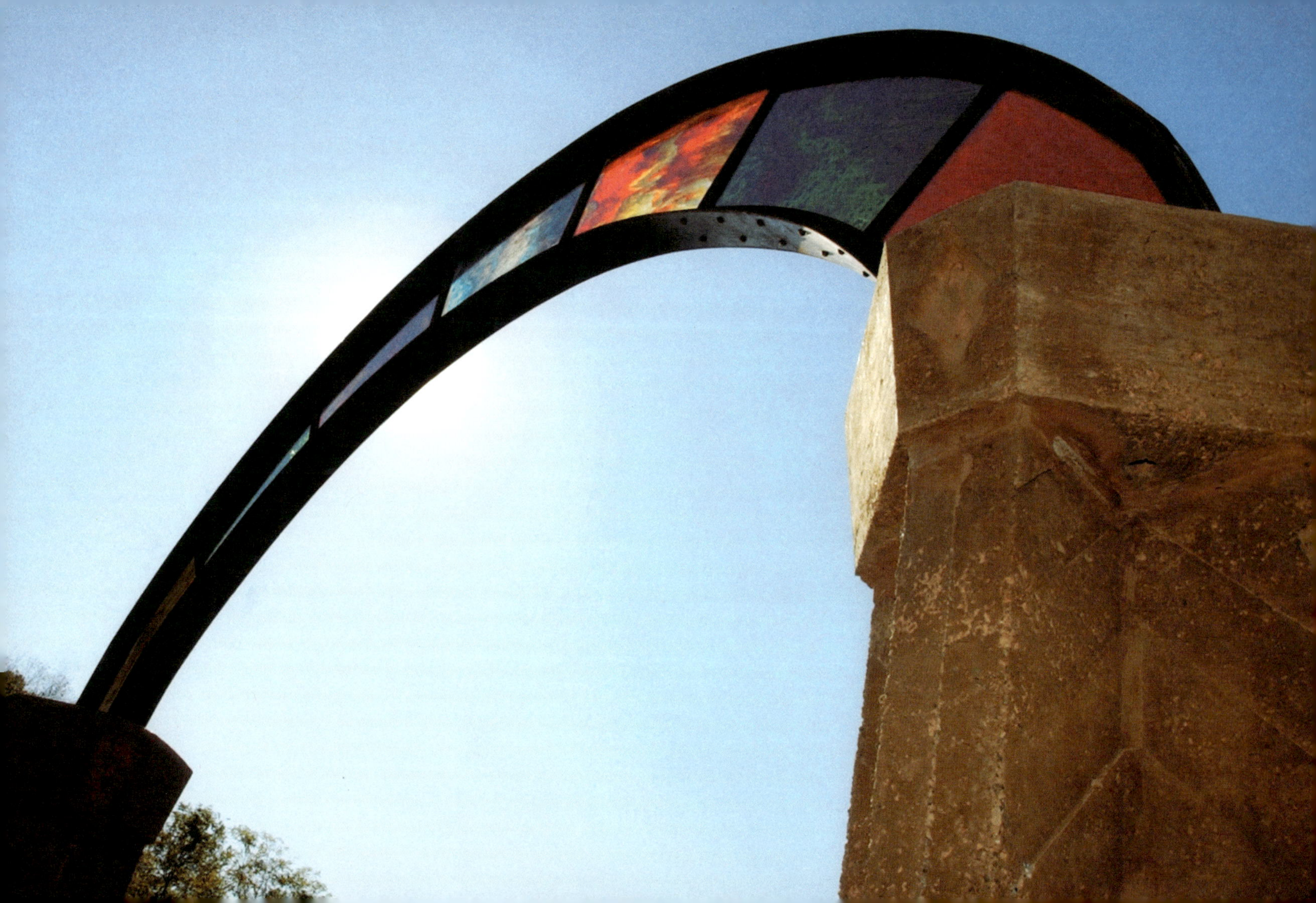

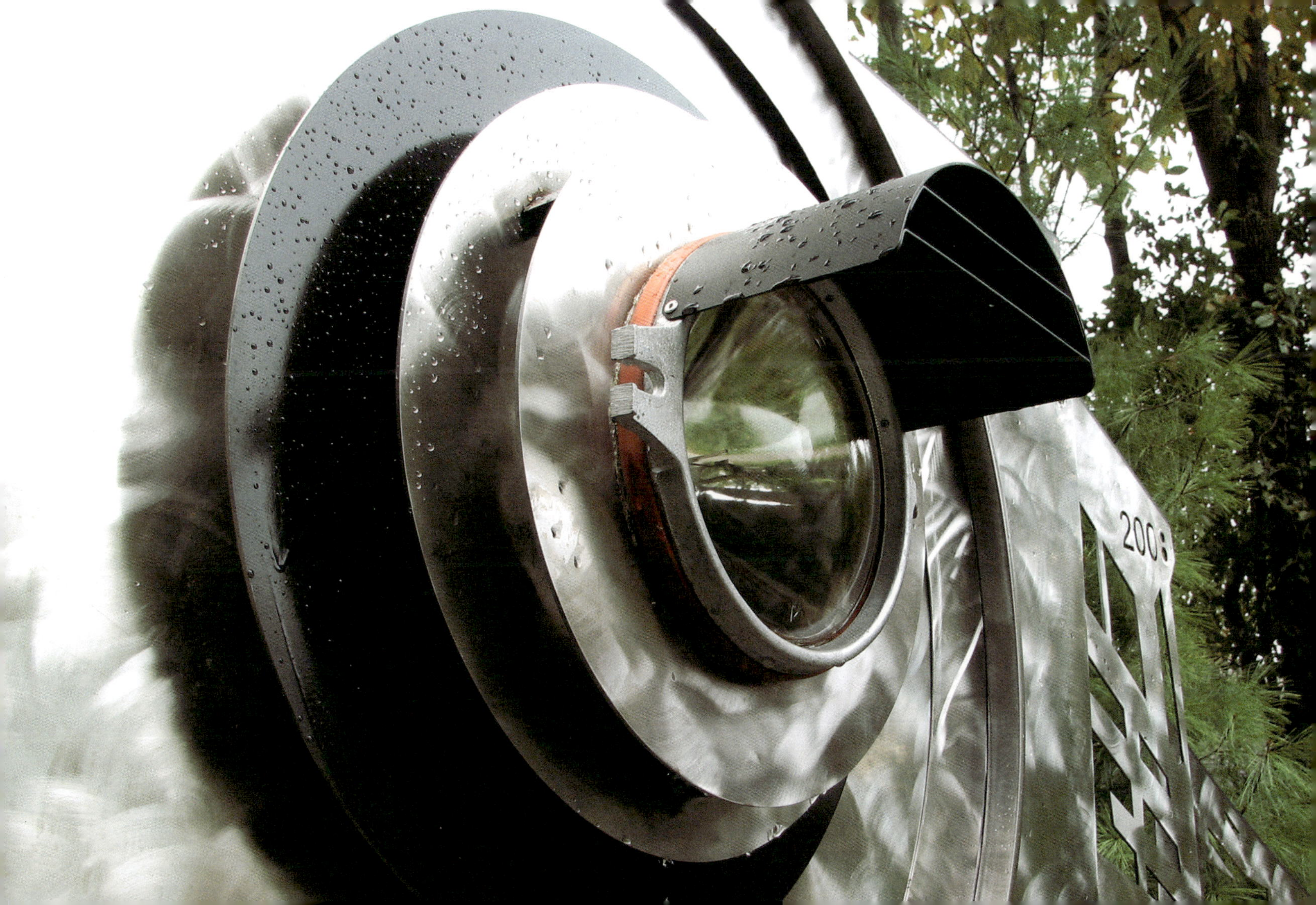
2008

John Stallings, Sculptor

Flood of Art

The intersection of Haynes and Napoleon Streets in the Kernville neighborhood of Johnstown is the second-busiest intersection in Cambria County. It's near the entrance to the city from Route 56—a route traveled by thousands every day, which makes husband-and-wife artists John and Cindy Stallings cringe, because the Haynes Street underpass is not pretty.

Neglect and population decline have made this location a renowned eyesore—which is one reason the Stallings targeted the intersection for the latest of John's public sculptures, a massive circular form planted in a tiny new parklet, sponsored in part by a Grassroots Grant from Community Connections.

"Kernville isn't just a blighted neighborhood," says Cindy Stallings, "it's the first impression of Johnstown—it's right off of the Route 56 exit. It's not only visitors' first sight, but thousands of Johnstowners themselves see it every day."

The Stallings weren't the only ones thinking about revitalizing Kernville with the arts. When John and Cindy began talks with the city about their public sculpture proposal, they discovered that Kernville had been designated for renovation through the Johnstown Artist Relocation Program.

Using public art to spur urban redevelopment isn't a new idea—it is, as an Americans for the Arts economic study determined in 2007, "an economically sound investment" for small towns as well as big cities, because "the arts mean business." The City of Johnstown has taken this idea to heart, targeting artists with financial subsidies, pre-arranged mortgages and other incentives to lure them into Kernville. With the Relocation Program in mind, the Stallings have ramped up their plan to include further sculptures in other strategic Kernville locations, commissioned from regional and national artists. "It's got to be something we'd consider 'museum-quality' artwork," says John Stallings. "And hopefully this will become known as a place to really show your work."

It's a plan that has attracted a lot of supporters. Since being awarded a Grassroots Grant, the Stallings' plan has seen other support come in from private companies as well as the Pennsylvania Rural Arts Alliance and the state's Department of Community and Economic Development. Meanwhile, John Stallings was named the sole recipient of 2008's George Sugarman Foundation grant, with the Foundation citing regional support for the Haynes Street project as an important part of their decision.

"This project's been a lesson in seeing things grow," says Cindy Stallings, "in how a seed can grow into something much bigger than we'd imagined. And in this case, the Community Connections grant was that seed."

03: HERITAGE

OUR HISTORIC FABRIC IS ONE THING OUR REGION REALLY HAS TO OFFER. BELIEVE ME; PEOPLE WILL BE INTERESTED IN THESE SITES IF THEY'RE BROUGHT BACK.

Restoration. Preservation. Legacy.

Map labels: Swamp; Juniata River; Fields cleared and plowed; Cliffs; Baker's Ovens; Gate; Road to Fort Pitt; Hospital; Storehouse

General Forbes made Raystown assembly point for English Provincial troops... west from Car[lisle] and north f[rom] Cumberland. [?] Soldiers [?]

In December of 1758 [a] successful expedition, [it would] be re-named "Fort Bedford." This fort is located on the [Juniata River?]

The main defence of this fort is [a stock]ade of vertical posts. On its north [side it] has the advantage of elevation above [the hil]ls along the Raystown branch of the...

Nº **54**/100 Old Bedford Village Redoubt and Encampment Awarded: $5,000

Southwestern Pennsylvania's daily life is informed by 250 years of history—whether it's Route 30 from Philadelphia to Pittsburgh, first cut by General Forbes in 1758, or the backdrop of industrial heritage found near Pittsburgh today. When it came time to acknowledge the region's 250th anniversary, naturally, many Community Connections projects incorporated history into their activities.

To some, the priority was on restoring and preserving physical artifacts like rescuing a 19th-century barn or preserving a restored theater from the Vaudeville Age. To others, it was the interpretation of history that mattered. For all of Community Connections' historical projects, the overarching theme was one of continuity between the past and the future—ensuring that the first 250 years remain a foundation on which the next 250 years can be built.

OLD BEDFORD VILLAGE
Motorcycling along the highways of Pennsylvania, Roger Kirwin sees the ghosts of Redcoats cutting paths across the state's landscape in 1758, laying the groundwork for a road still traveled today.

"The French and Indian War was all about movement," says Kirwin, executive director of Old Bedford Village, the living-history center on the site of the 18th-century fortress in Bedford County. "It was about, 'How do you move 7,000 soldiers back and forth across the state's woodlands?' And when you move around Pennsylvania today, you trace those movements. Look just off the turnpike, and you see woodlands that aren't much different than they were 250 years ago. There are very few places left where you can look at history like that."

What's not always so apparent is *which* history is on display at the Village. Despite the center's direct link to the French and Indian War, visitors are just as likely to encounter people dressed in Confederate gray or Napoleonic-era uniforms.

"The thing about Old Bedford Village is its versatility," says Kirwin, known to don a red coat himself as a French and Indian War reenactor. And it's towards that end that the Village was awarded a Grassroots Grant to build its new *pan coupe redan*—a type of defensive structure used in the U.S. and Europe from the 1750s through the early-20th century.

With the *redan*'s addition, Old Bedford Village solidified itself as a premier location for living historians, no matter what era they cast themselves in. Those historians and hobbyists

Old Bedford Village *redan*, Bedford County

have responded in kind. Not only did groups of reenactors aid in the construction of the *redan*, the structure has attracted attention from hundreds who gleefully used this newly-added authenticity and attended 2008's celebrations of Bedford's 250th anniversary. And drawing those people to Bedford, says Kirwin, makes the Village a more dynamic educational and cultural amenity.

"When you can bring the places and characters of history to life, the public gets more interested," says Kirwin. "It takes things out of the realm of academia and into a tactile, tangible understanding of history. We give living historians a marvelous canvas for reenactments, and, in return, they come here and give the public something to see."

BARN STORMING

Whenever Jack Maguire saw a historic building in Saltsburg, Indiana County, threatened with demolition, he had a simple solution: Buy it. A commercial building from 1913, the old Academy built in 1851, the town's high school—each time one of these buildings was targeted by the wrecking ball, Maguire bought it, refurbished it, and found contemporary uses that maintain the historical integrity of the building.

When talk began about pulling down the circa-1850 W.R. McIlwain Store and Warehouse, Maguire knew there'd be little public outcry. Because of its positioning along the once-busy canal, the dilapidated building has long been known by the less-than-impressive misnomer, "The Mule Barn," as such buildings were common as housing for the animals that towed boats on the canal. (The fact that this storehouse likely never served that purpose is a moot point. As any Western Pennsylvanian can tell you, once a place is named, it stays named.)

A run-down local eyesore with "mule" in its name? Maguire knew that it'd take stubborn determination to win this one.

"It just doesn't look good," says Maguire, a semi-retired civil engineer and lifelong Saltsburg resident. "There'd been a fire at the back of the main structure, and the roof was collapsing. But, in my mind's eye, I can see how it'd look if it was restored. And in Saltsburg, what you've got to do is just step forward and do the work—don't just talk about it."

Which is just what Maguire did: He volunteered to tear down the rear section of the Barn, to help "some of those eyesore complaints go away." With a Grassroots Grant acquired by Saltsburg Borough, Maguire and other volunteers stabilized the Barn, which had been listing to one side.

To Maguire and fellow preservationists, The Mule Barn represents an important part of Saltsburg's history, dating from the mid-19th century when the Harrisburg-to-Pittsburgh canal went through town and beasts of burden pulled the barges. As Saltsburg Borough President Elizabeth Rocco says, were the Barn to go, "that'd be just one more piece of our history that we'll never get back."

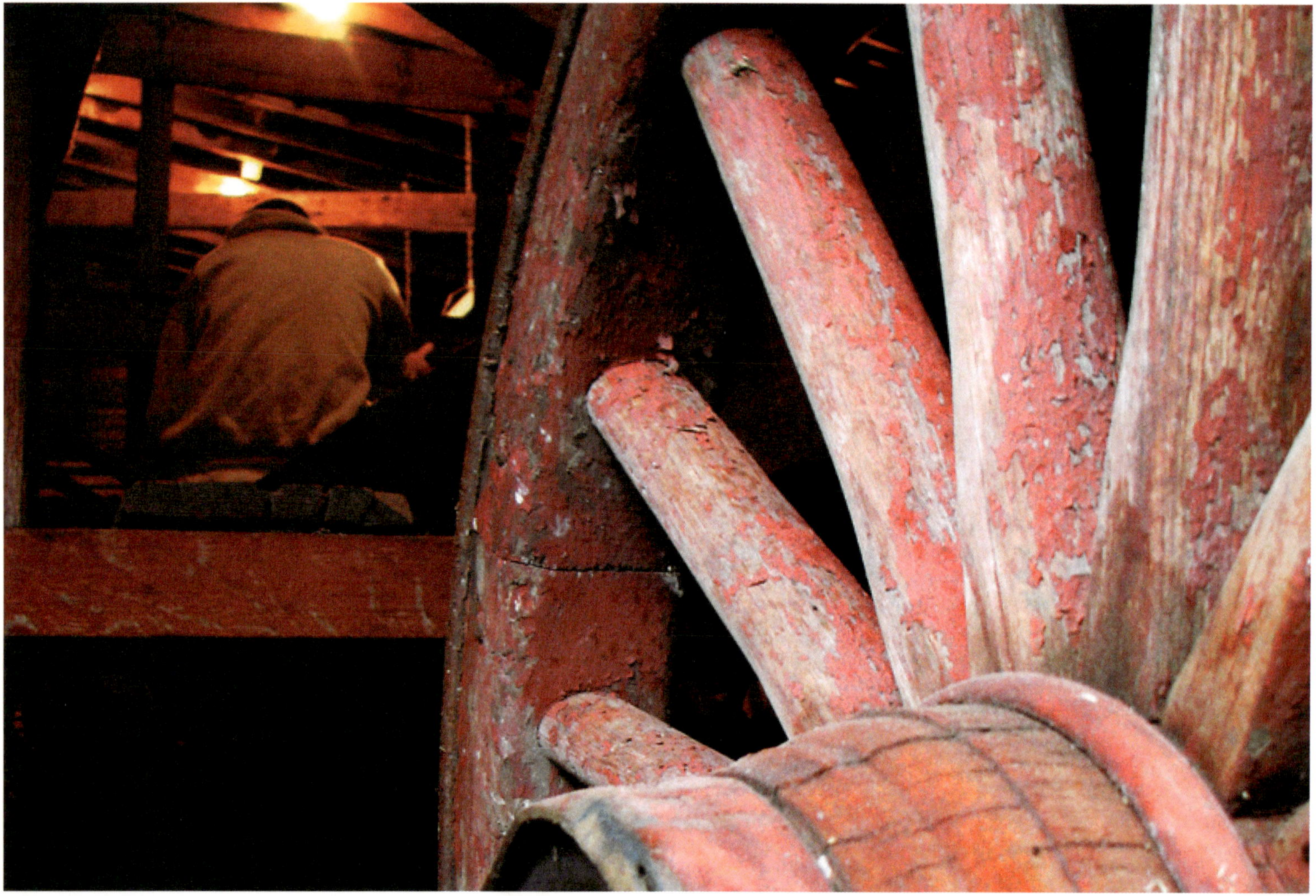

It's all part of what Jack Maguire calls "our historic fabric"—the future of which is in our hands. "History is one thing we really have to offer," says Maguire. "And, believe me: people will be interested in these sites if they're brought back."

RE-COVERED WAGON

At the 50-acre Succop Conservancy, located on Route 8 just a few miles south of Butler, Director Nancy Lawry points out a former incubator from this property's past as a chicken farm—now it's a blacksmith's shop for the Conservancy's Heritage School. Here, no space or material is wasted: The previous owner's swimming pool, filled in for safety reasons, became an herb garden; its bathhouse, the kitchen for outdoor events, refurbished with timber from cleared acreage.

This philosophy goes hand-in-hand with the Conservancy's establishing directive, as laid out by Tom and JoAnn Succop when they donated their family farmland in 2001, to keep the land for education and environmental stewardship purposes in perpetuity.

So when the Conservancy pulled a pre-Civil War hay wagon from the farm's early-19th century barn, it was only natural that its restoration should become part of the Conservancy's mission. That didn't mean the task would be easy. "It was in a dark corner of the barn, with a family of raccoons living in it," says Lawry. "It's hard to even think back to what it looked like."

With help from a Grassroots Grant, the Conservancy assembled a Venturing Crew—a team of teenagers, working through Boy Scouts of America. With the Conservancy's woodworking expert and blacksmith, that crew restored the wagon—forging new wheel spokes to replace broken ones, and touching up and painting the wooden frame. In the process, the crew learned hands-on lessons about how agricultural Butler was built 100 years ago.

It's just the sort of skills that visitors will learn at the Heritage School, a new initiative that makes Succop Conservancy a destination for historical folk-trade education. Classes range from blacksmithing and woodworking to aromatherapy and Native American storytelling.

The wagon now plays an integral role in the life of the Conservancy, acting as its icon and a working transport for students, the Venturing Crew, or anyone participating in community activities like Butler County's Master Gardeners events.

But perhaps the most important aspect of the project is the ongoing restoration work itself, illustrating the experiences of our ancestors.

"We've got the ability to use the wagon for community events, and for rides," says Lawry. "But more than that, it's just an important reminder of the farming heritage that made this area—and our country—what it is today."

THEATER DREAMS

When Denise Mihalick walks the aisles of the Arcadia Theater, built in 1921, she follows in famed footsteps: movie star Loretta Young, for example, and Depression-era film star Joan Blondell, both paced the Arcadia's stage in its vaudeville days according to tickets stubs found in the building.

But as executive director of the Arcadia, located in Windber, Somerset County, Mihalick tempers those dreams of its heyday with nightmares of its dilapidated recent past. Photos of the Arcadia prior to its 1998 restoration show an interior brutally wracked by age and neglect, its ceilings caved in, its walls crumbling under their own weight.

Fortunately, today's Arcadia is full of past glory. Restored to its gilded-age appearance, based on artifacts as small as a piece of long-gone carpeting or a photograph highlighting an exterior feature, the Theater is once again the crown jewel of the Windber area. And, with the recent memory of the Arcadia's dilapidation in tow, Mihalick says the community is committed to keeping it that way. "The people of Windber are so proud of this theater," says Mihalick. "To give you an example, I am the only paid employee—the entire theater is run by volunteers, from the box office to the ushers."

Today, the Arcadia Theater has the success it needs to keep operating: According to Mihalick, monthly performances regularly sell out the 690-seat theater. But while ticket sales and sponsorships cover production expenses, the Arcadia's needs for future renovation and preservation are, so far, unfunded.

"The building is 96 years old—we need a new roof, and everything from the constant need to upgrade technical equipment, to slowly replacing all the toilets. If we can raise enough money to start a sizable endowment, we'll live off the interest whenever we need some capital improvements."

With the help of a Grassroots Grant, the Arcadia kicked off its endowment campaign on October 25, 2008—nearly ten years to the day after its first post-restoration performance.

"We've become regional," says Mihalick. "From Johnstown to Somerset to Altoona, our reputation isn't just the quality and diversity of entertainment, but the warmth—the magical appearance of the theater. It's referred to as the 'gem of the area,' but it's not just the theater—when we have show nights, every restaurant is full, everything's busy. And that can't help but give visibility to the town."

The anniversary fundraising gala was just a first step toward ensuring the lasting legacy of the Arcadia Theatre. And, if Mihalick has anything to do with it, there will be many more steps to come.

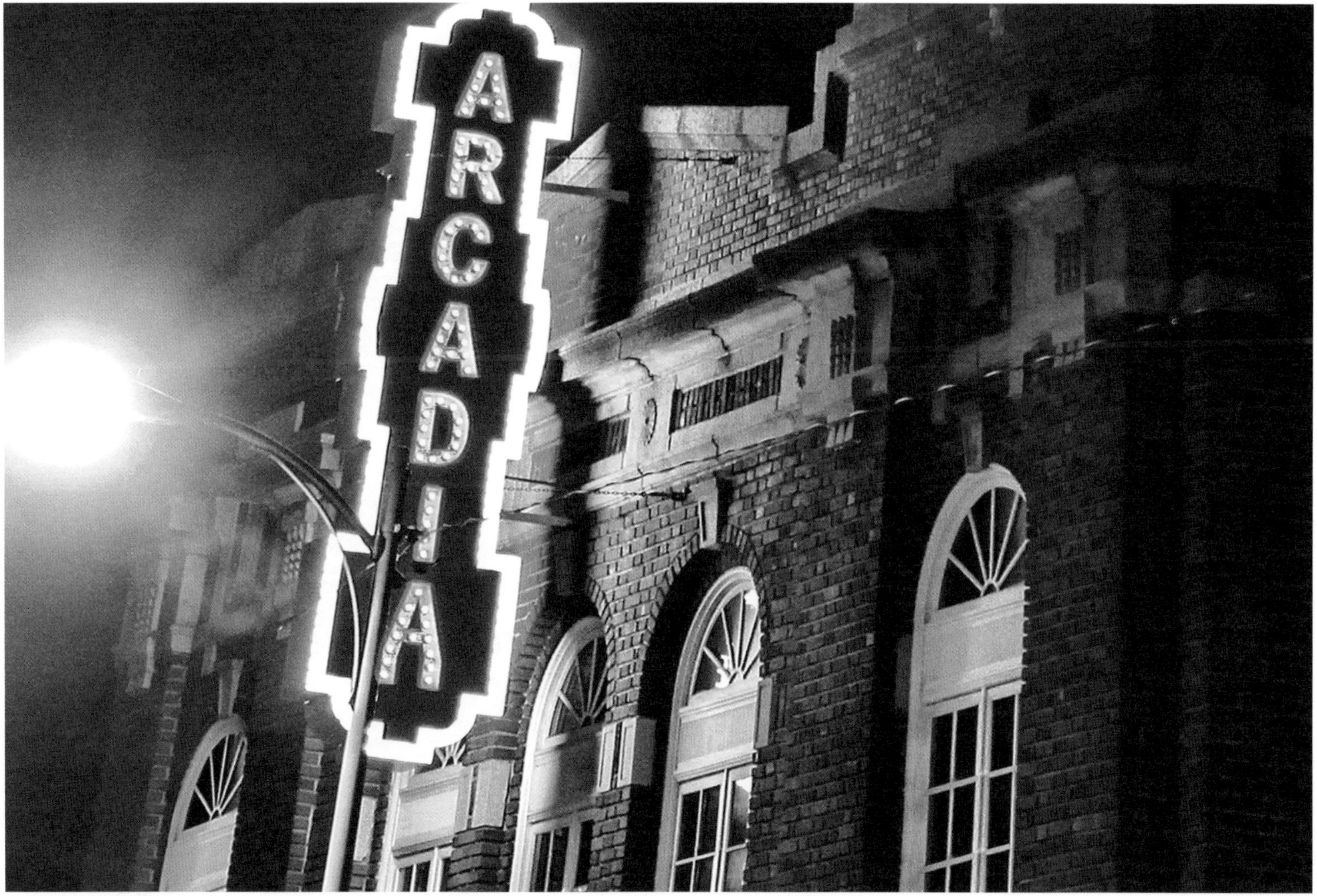
ARCADIA

№: 47\100   **First Company Fort McIntosh Garrison Revitalization**   Awarded: $5,000

Life in the Past Lane

A burly, buck-skinned businessman stops through this territory frequently, setting up the tented trading post that displays his wares: muskets, ammunition, pipes and blankets, whatever the natives want in trade for the beaver and deer furs they've got in plenty. He might be based out of Fort Pitt, like so many traveling traders, but he doesn't spend much time there—more often it's North to the Iroquois or West to the Shawnee, to see what he can rustle up.

This is, of course, spinning a bit of a yarn—after all, it's 2008, not 1758. But it's easy to get caught up and forget that this is Boyce Park in Allegheny County—and that there's a swing set just around the bend. The trading post is, in fact, just a stop along the trail of Washington's Encampment, a Grassroots Project that brought 1758 to life for thousands of visitors from around the region and beyond.

During the Pittsburgh Celebrates 250 weekend, October 4–5, the Allegheny Foothills Historical Society took over Boyce Park in Plum Borough, turning it into an encampment based on that of General John Forbes and Colonel George Washington in the fall of 1758, when the two prepared to march into what is now Pittsburgh. Hundreds of French and Indian War reenactors—from Redcoats and George Washington to Native Americans and fur traders—converged on Washington's Encampment, to illustrate the people and events that cut the Pittsburgh region as we know it out of the wilderness.

As Washington's Encampment was underway, the Fort McIntosh Garrison was gearing up for an 18th-century event of its own. The Beaver County living-history unit, which specializes in the latter part of that century—and Western Pennsylvania's Revolutionary War era—was badly in need of a refitting. (The 2008 economic crisis took its toll on gunpowder and uniform prices, too.) With a Grassroots Grant, the unit reorganized and revitalized its tools of the trade, debuting its new, historically accurate materials at an event in October.

The experience of living-history events such as Washington's Encampment and Fort McIntosh is not so much immersion as it is education—a fact that rang out clearly. The kids started getting their basics straight—"Why were their guns so long?" "I thought the Redcoats were the bad guys?" Even some of the know-it-alls got schooled, too, in everything from the simple inner workings of a musket, to the complex intersection of historical changes—involving wealthy British industrialists and lowly North American fur traders alike—that illustrate how Pittsburgh came to be.

THE FRENCH AND INDIAN WAR WAS ALL ABOUT MOVEMENT. AND WHEN YOU MOVE AROUND PENNSYLVANIA TODAY, YOU TRACE THOSE MOVEMENTS. YOU SEE WOODLANDS THAT AREN'T MUCH DIFFERENT THAN THEY WERE 250 YEARS AGO. THERE ARE VERY FEW PLACES LEFT WHERE YOU CAN LOOK AT HISTORY LIKE THAT.

№:**35**\100 **Washington's Encampment**   Awarded: $5,000

04: **LANDSCAPE**

ON THE SURFACE, WE'RE CLEANING UP THE COMMUNITY, BUT WHAT WE'RE REALLY DOING IS BUILDING SOCIAL CAPITAL. WHEN PEOPLE COME AND PARTICIPATE, THEY SEE OUR NEIGHBORHOOD IN A DIFFERENT LIGHT.

Appearance. Beautification. Pride.

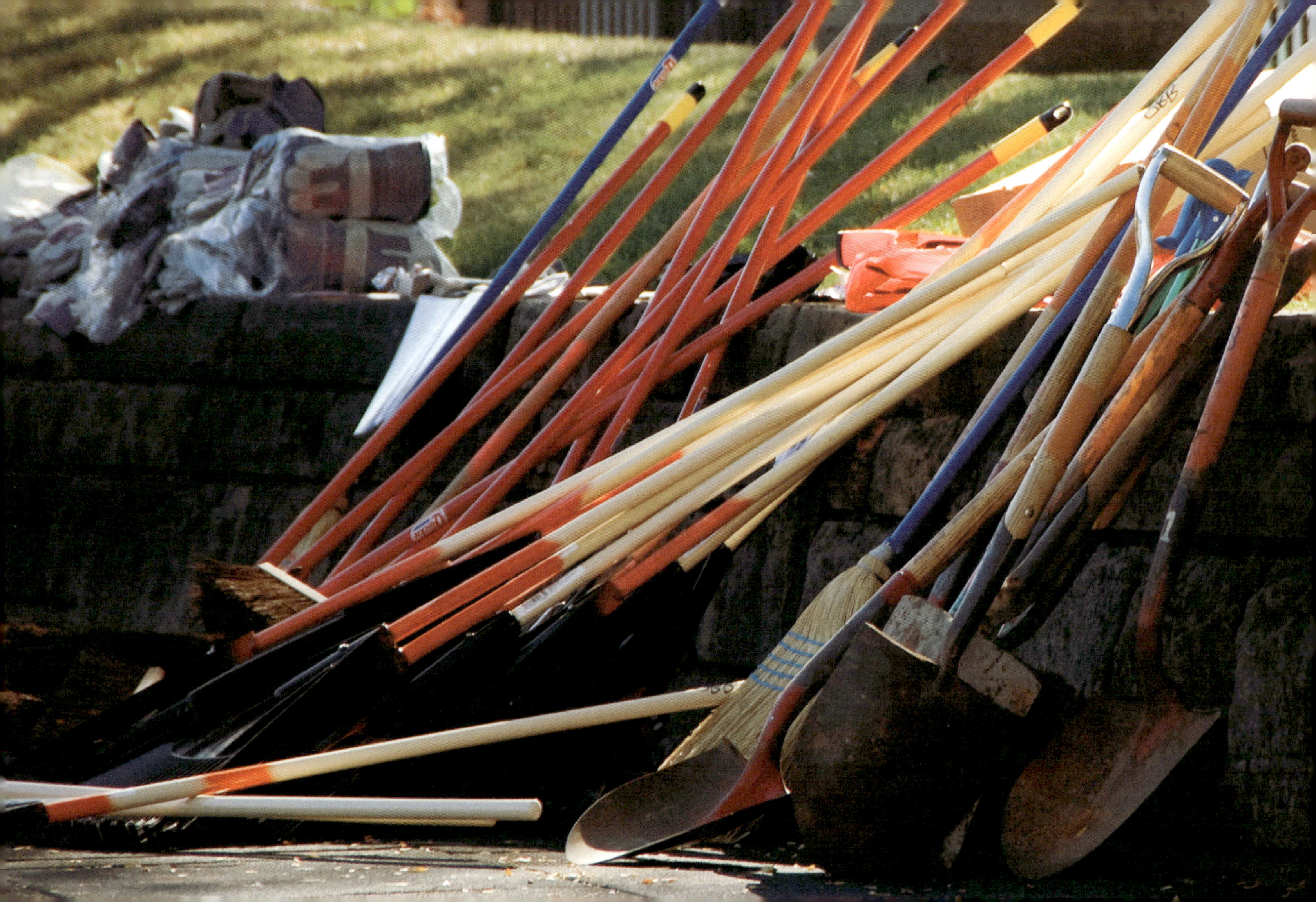

Unlike some community projects, revitalization efforts often come with the satisfying immediacy of a visible result. There are statistically calculable and physically tangible outcomes— 16 tons of garbage picked up by one Homewood clean-up; a new green space to accompany the nascent library in Millvale; a blueprint to work from in a new Johnstown recreational area.

Khalif Ali, Homewood
Community Organizer

But when Khalif Ali grins his satisfied smile, it's about something more than the garbage bags—stuffed full and piled high—collected by the volunteers at his Homewood Redd Up. And not just any patch of grass can make Brian Wolovich beam with pride, only one with as much history behind it as Millvale's. Ali, Wolovich, and community organizers around the region spend their weekends changing the appearance of their neighborhoods not just to make them look different, but to change the way they're viewed. And, by reshaping that vision, Community Connections became a way to change the expectations of residents and visitors alike.

IN A DIFFERENT LIGHT

Standing on a small park embankment in Pittsburgh's Homewood neighborhood, Khalif Ali—a coordinator with a local community organization, Operation Better Block—clutches a microphone like a natural. Organizing his small army of volunteers, Ali isn't so much general as master of ceremonies, elevating his orders—the distribution of work gloves, rakes, industrial-strength garbage bags—into a kind of Saturday morning stage patter. "Yeah, I know," he says, smiling to the assemblage, "I love the mic."

The crowd Ali addresses is eccentric: blurry-eyed college students stand beside senior citizens and community activists. The ringleader of one Homewood church group nudges City Councilman Bill Peduto about a few of the community's needs, while members of a University of Pittsburgh fraternity collect the tools they'll need to join in the day's Homewood Redd Up—the biannual community clean-up (named for the Pittsburgh-via-Scotland colloquialism meaning "to tidy up"), sponsored in 2008 by a Grassroots Grant. Unlike some Pittsburgh neighborhoods, cleaning up Homewood isn't just a battle against litter, as Ali's instructions illustrate.

"Make sure your group has one of these syringe bottles," Ali announces. "You'll need them when you find needles—and you *will* find needles."

Homewood is a tough neighborhood, beset by poverty, drugs, and gangs, and cleaning it up requires a passionate dedication. Operation Better Block joined forces with organizations in more affluent East End neighborhoods to form the Homewood-Squirrel Hill-Point Breeze Redd Up Coalition. The coalition brought people together from neighborhoods that might be only a few blocks apart geographically, but sometimes seem worlds apart culturally. As Executive Director Aliya Durham explains, the Redd Up is about so much more than just clean streets and parks.

"On the surface, we're cleaning up the community, but what we're really doing is building social capital," says Durham. "Afterwards, while volunteers share lunch together, they're talking to one another—it raises the visibility of our neighborhood; shows that there are so many good people who live here. When people come and participate, they see our neighborhood in a different light."

It's not just volunteers from all over the East End that get a new picture of Homewood thanks to the Redd Up; Homewood residents—from all walks of life—get a different view of their neighborhood when they see their neighbors and fellow Pittsburghers investing in the community. Durham recounts one story of a senior citizen from Squirrel Hill assigned to clean a particularly "tough intersection, with open drug dealing."

"I know the neighborhood, and I was uncomfortable with where she was," says Durham. "I stopped to check on her, and she said some guys had come out on the corner, 'But I talked to them and told them I needed to clean it up, and they moved out of the way.'"

When people from other places show an interest in a neighborhood, it changes the psychology of the whole community.

"And that," says Durham, "changes everything."

CAMBRIAN GARDEN

There is a folktale that persists from the glory days of Ebensburg—the late-19th-century period when the small Cambria County town, 30 miles north of Johnstown, served as summer home and getaway for the robber barons of Pittsburgh. Looking over the workers preparing her garden for a wedding, an aristocratic matriarch announced from her porch, "Cut the hedges low so that the natives may watch."

Walking through the doors of the Cambria County Historical Society's museum, visitors encounter this folktale inscribed on a card and posted near the museum's entrance. Which is appropriate, if tongue-in-cheek: It's with a similar mission, though from a more populist perspective, that the Society invites "the natives" into the magnificent A.W. Buck House for a new exhibit of Ebensburg's history.

Welcoming visitors to the building are the carefully trimmed hedges of the site's new Victorian-era garden—recreated in detail from period photographs by Kendall-O'Brien, a Pittsburgh-based firm of landscape architects with ties to Ebensburg, with help from a Grassroots Grant.

N°: **66**\100   **Planting Connections: Our Cambrian Garden**   Awarded: $5,000

The house was purchased by the Society in 1990—after 50 years as a private home, and 50 years as a convent. But while the interior was restored to its 19th-century state in 2000, the house's exterior remained staunchly 20th-century—an annoyance to an organization intent on replication of a historical era.

"None of the period photos show the whole yard, but from other artifacts you get a good picture of it," says Historical Society Secretary Dave Huber. "We have an etching of the house from 1890, with a lot of detail. You can see the courtyard centerpiece, and the whole property had a six-foot-tall wrought-iron fence."

The fence, hedges, and courtyard have all been recreated from the pieced-together surviving images. The courtyard, crowned by an arbor under which visitors now enter, and containing iron benches and lawn urns, has become the focal point of the museum's exterior, and provides an outdoor setting in which visitors can gather. It has another purpose, as well: to aesthetically connect the Buck House to Ebensburg's downtown, just six blocks away.

"We really strived to tie this in to the recent downtown revitalization, which had a Victorian theme," says Huber. "Similar trees, similar iron work—we're hoping that will help lead people into the museum from downtown."

BRIDGE TO THE FUTURE

It was a seemingly minor incident that brought change to the small Beaver County borough of Ambridge. In 2006, the borough's lone street sweeper broke down, leaving the tenants of Ambridge's Merchant Street business district to watch as leaves and litter piled up. Rebecca Sciulli-Carlson and her family were among those business owners.

"I'm tethered to Ambridge," says Sciulli-Carlson. "My family owns a small appliance business—we've operated it for four generations now. And when the street sweeper broke, everyone was lamenting it—so we just started going out there every Sunday and cleaning a mile and a half of Merchant Street, just walking block-by-block."

It would be hard to find an example of post-industrial America more poetic than that of Ambridge: Employment and living standards dropped sharply there in the 1970s, culminating in 1983's closing of American Bridge's operations, the company for which Ambridge was named. What followed were two decades of rethinking by politicians and community activists, a process that Sciulli-Carlson believes has now led to the current plan to revitalize using brownfield spaces such as the location of the former H.H. Robinson steel mill. With recent international investments by Australian entrepreneur Robert Moltoni, Sciulli-Carson says, "People in Ambridge began to think, 'yes, we really can change our future.'"

PŒONIA. (MOUTAN) ELIZABETH CASORETTI.

So when the newly dubbed Committee to Clean and Beautify Ambridge hit the streets to clean up each Sunday, other Ambridge locals began joining in. The group's ranks swelled from five initial volunteers to its current membership of over 30, and when the street sweeper came back online, the organization—with Sciulli-Carlson as its chair—began looking for other opportunities.

"We began looking at the gateways to Ambridge, with help from Western Pennsylvania Conservancy," says Sciulli-Carlson. First, the group built up the park space around a World War II-era anchor positioned near the entrance into town from Route 65. Then the Conservancy suggested adding a water feature at P.J. Caul Park, another heavily trafficked gateway into the city. "We said, 'yeah—a water feature,'" laughs Sciulli-Carlson. "We couldn't afford the plastic bags we were using for trash!"

So the Committee continued building relationships— with businesses like Value Ambridge Properties and the New Economy Business Park, that had an interest in revitalizing the communities they serve, and with public entities such as Pennsylvania Department of Transportation, which contributes materials to the organization.

Now, according to Sciulli-Carlson, over 100 people are directly or indirectly involved in working with the organization. And when Pittsburgh 250 was announced, the Committee secured a Grassroots Grant to finally finish their second "Gateway to Ambridge," complete with a refreshing water sculpture. The rest of the park came together with hours upon hours of volunteer time from the community, including substantial overtime from the water feature's builder, Ambridge resident Rob DeMacio. And that community participation is, perhaps, the most important part.

"It's had such a positive response from the whole community," says Sciulli-Carlson, "and, as a result, it encourages others to do the same kind of thing."

THE DOMINO EFFECT

Millvale resident Brian Wolovich can rattle off a list of local cultural landmarks befitting a town twice its size. "We've got Pittsburgh's best French bakery; Kitman's famous furniture store; the Lincoln Diner—where Pamela's restaurants started; Riverfront Park; The Attic record store and Mr. Small's Theater, which are both world famous."

But Wolovich, a teacher at Quaker Valley Middle School, will also be the first to tell you what this Allegheny River town just outside Pittsburgh is lacking—and it's a list at least as long. Besides the dwindling population, loss of businesses, and unemployment common to many similar former mill towns, much of Millvale sits in a flood plain.

"When Hurricane Ivan hit in 2004, we had everyone from local government to George W. Bush come here and make promises," says Wolovich—but much like Katrina in the Gulf Coast, the real shock was the lack of help afterwards.

№: **22**\100   **Grant Avenue Pocket Park**   Awarded: $5,000

Standing inside Red Star Ironworks, Brian Wolovich smiles at the thought of New Sun Rising's new parklet on Grant Avenue, the main drag in his beloved Millvale, Allegheny County. With local partners like the renowned artisans at Red Star, who fabricated the fittings for the new park, Wolovich's organization has bolstered its signature Millvale Library project with efforts to revitalize the image—and the self-confidence—of a town that has survived industrial demise and a constant battle against floodwaters. As befits its history and its proudly stubborn population, even the town's park—an oasis of green amongst the bustling grey of Millvale's post-industrial patch—is reinforced with iron and built to last.

"Everyone came back again after the floods in August of 2007. At least that woke up the media, asking why those 2004 promises weren't kept."

That's why Wolovich joined with a few friends and family members to form New Sun Rising, a nonprofit organization with lofty goals to revitalize Millvale—most notably, creating the Millvale Library, which began operating in the summer of 2008. But while the impact of Millvale having its own local library is obvious, another aspect of the project takes a more subtle tact. With the Grant Avenue Pocket Park, funded by a Grassroots Grant, New Sun Rising has opened up a patch of park land near the library, in the middle of Millvale's business district.

"Millvale's not the most relaxing place in the world," says Wolovich. "The best amenity we have is Riverfront Park, but it's severed from the community by Route 28, a busy four-lane highway. The green space will have so many benefits, but most of all, it's just a place for people to relax."

Like the Homewood Redd Up, the library and green space have provided opportunities to show residents and visitors a new face of Millvale. New Sun Rising has hosted volunteers from as far away as Florida to work on its projects, besides bringing together local activists and community organizers to see the potential that Millvale holds. Beyond simply providing a breather for people already in the community, Wolovich sees the green space as the next stage in building a new Millvale—a place that can take advantage of its low cost

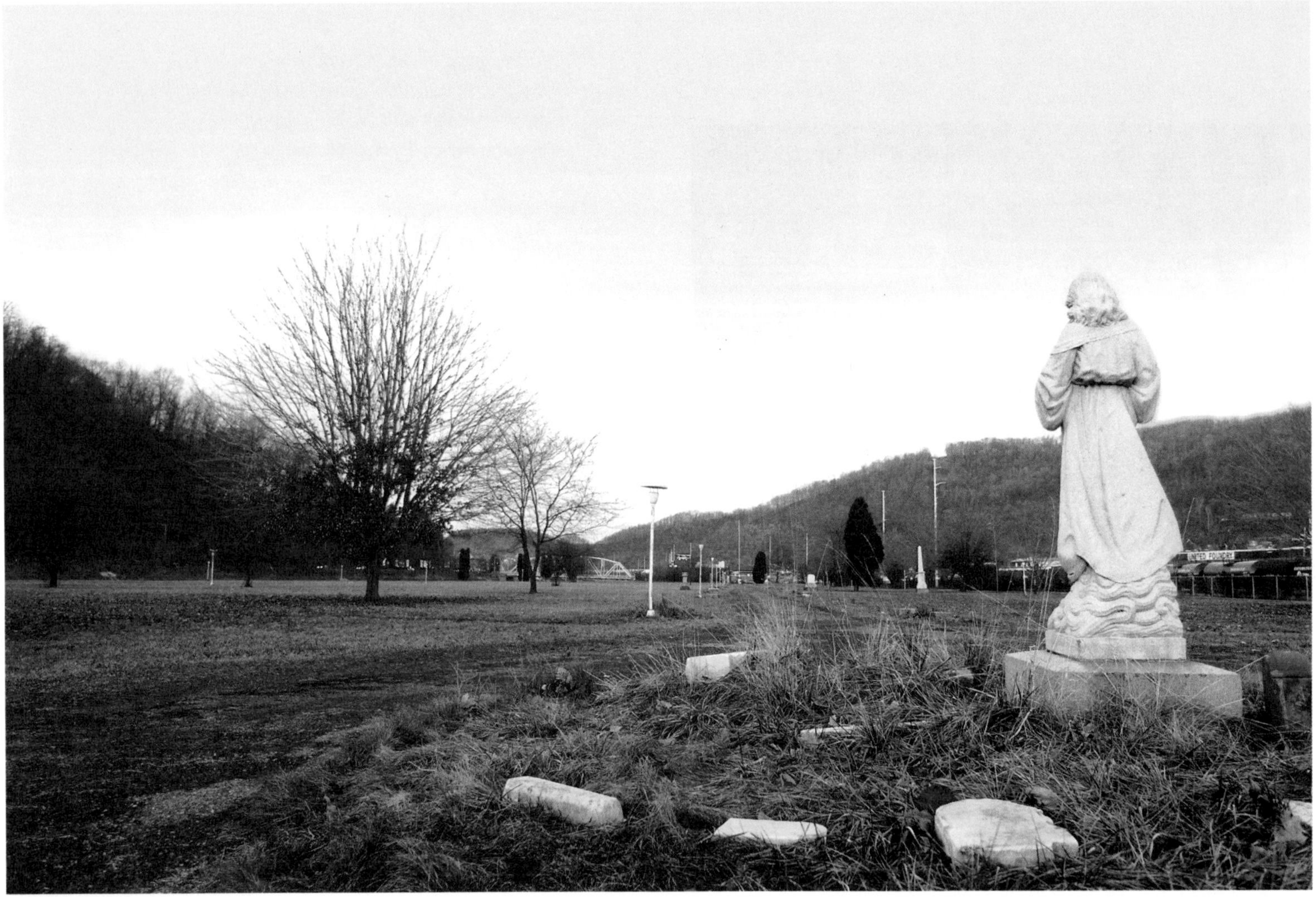
UNITED FOUNDRY

of living and opportunities for home ownership, and begin to bring new families into the community to buy houses and invest in the neighborhood.

"If you buy it, you care for it more," says Wolovich. "Millvale has a much higher-than-average percentage of renters, so you see houses falling into disrepair. I think combinations like the library and the green space, they impact people's interest in buying into the community. Young families can afford to buy a house here, so I see it having a domino effect."

A JOB BEGUN

Bill Horner passes his hand along a worn gravestone, reading the words as he touches them: "Jacob Horner," he says. "Founder and Proprietor of Sandyvale Cemetery."

The shared surname is no coincidence, nor is the name of the location—Sandyvale sits in a neighborhood of Johnstown, Cambria County, called Hornerstown, named for Bill's ancestors, including Jacob. Although burials here date back to the Revolutionary War era, the other gravestones at Sandyvale are few in number and random in location—the result of Johnstown's famous floods in 1889, 1936, and 1977. A few trees and some weathered statuary dot the landscape, where dog-walkers and joggers frequent circular paved trails at lunchtime.

Standing in the middle of Sandyvale Cemetery Memorial Garden there's little to signal the ambitious changes that Horner, Diana Kabo, and the rest of the Sandyvale Cemetery Association board members have in mind for this plot of hallowed ground. But Sandyvale is about to see its landscape overhauled again—this time, not by the chaos of floodwaters, but by careful planning executed by dedicated stewards.

The plans for Sandyvale are remarkable. There's a hiking-and-biking trail that runs along the Cemetery's perimeter to link up with established trails such as the Path of the Flood Trail and the James Mayer Riverwalk. A disused barn at the land's edge, donated to the Association, is ready to be transformed into a visitor's center. And long-range plans include multiple botanical gardens and an arboretum. To Horner, it's all part of a renaissance in Johnstown.

"This is a city in transition," says Horner. "Steel's gone, coal is somewhat gone, now it's defense and information technology that run this area. But people are really taken with the quality of life here, and that's what this project impacts."

Horner and Kabo stress that the master plan they've produced will take years to complete. But thanks in part to a Grassroots Grant to get 2008's planning phase and initial work underway, Bill Horner can already imagine his predecessors' glee.

"What we needed was to start," says Horner. It's a sentiment echoed throughout community efforts working to revitalize through beautification—from Allegheny to Beaver to Cambria and beyond.

"It's like my father always used to say," says Horner, "'A job begun is a job half done.'"

№: **41**\100 **Postage Stamp Park** Awarded: $5,000

There was no ribbon at the "ribbon-cutting" for the new Postage Stamp Park in Parker, Armstrong County. Instead, members of the Parker City Revitalization Corporation sliced through black-and-gold caution tape to signify the opening of the tiny park in October 2008. Postage Stamp is no misnomer for the park, just a dozen people wide, sandwiched between the Allegheny River and North River Avenue. But a few tables, a bench, and a spectacular view are all you need to step off one of the multiple hiking or biking trails that cross near Parker, or pull ashore to take a breather in "America's Smallest City."

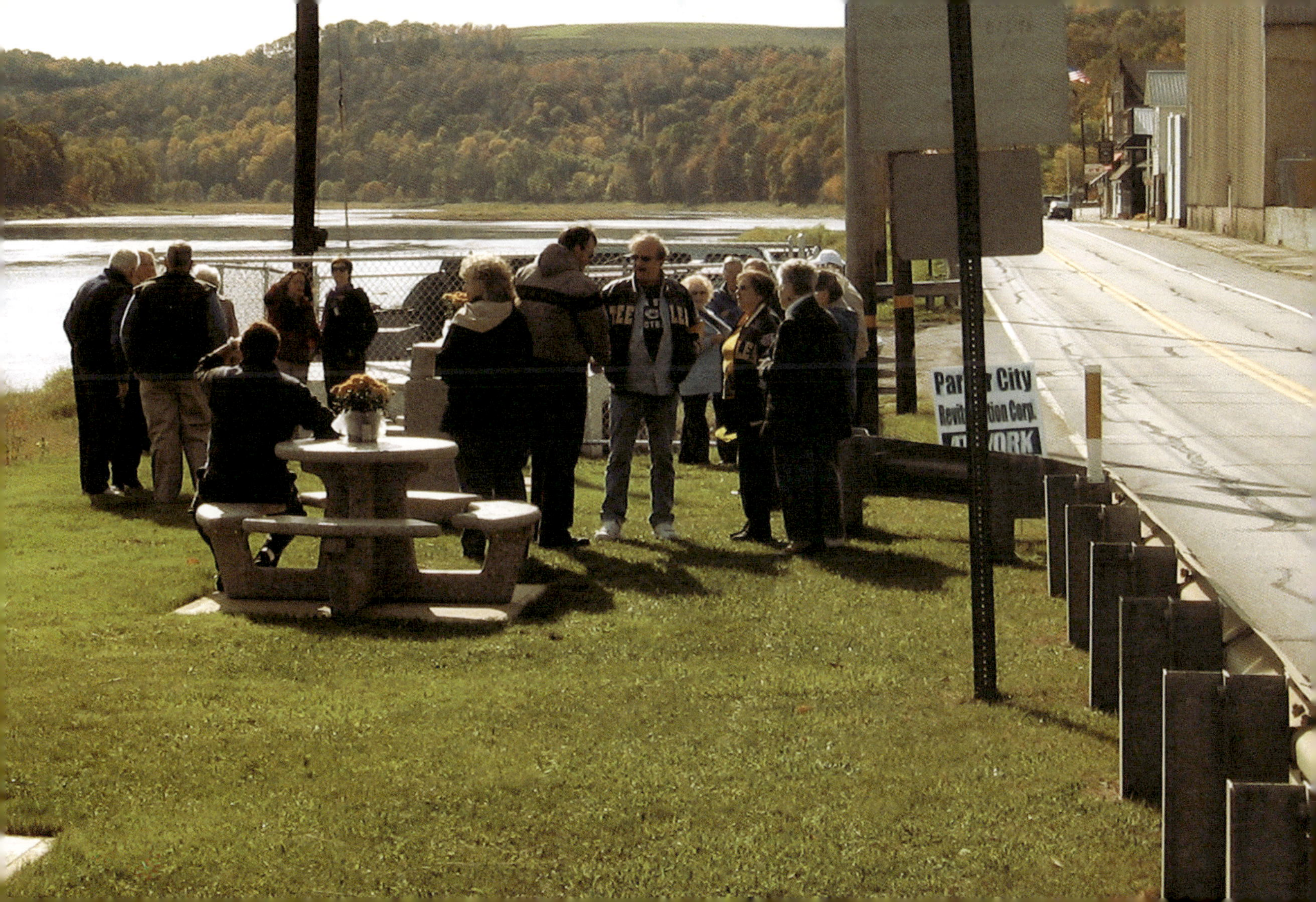
City
Corp.
ORK

05: **CHARACTER**

SOMETHING THAT REALLY STANDS OUT ABOUT PITTSBURGH IS THAT ALL OF THE NEIGHBORHOODS HAVE A UNIQUE IDENTITY, AND PITTSBURGHERS HAVE SO MUCH PRIDE IN THAT INDIVIDUAL IDENTITY AND EXPERIENCE.

History. Culture. Understanding.

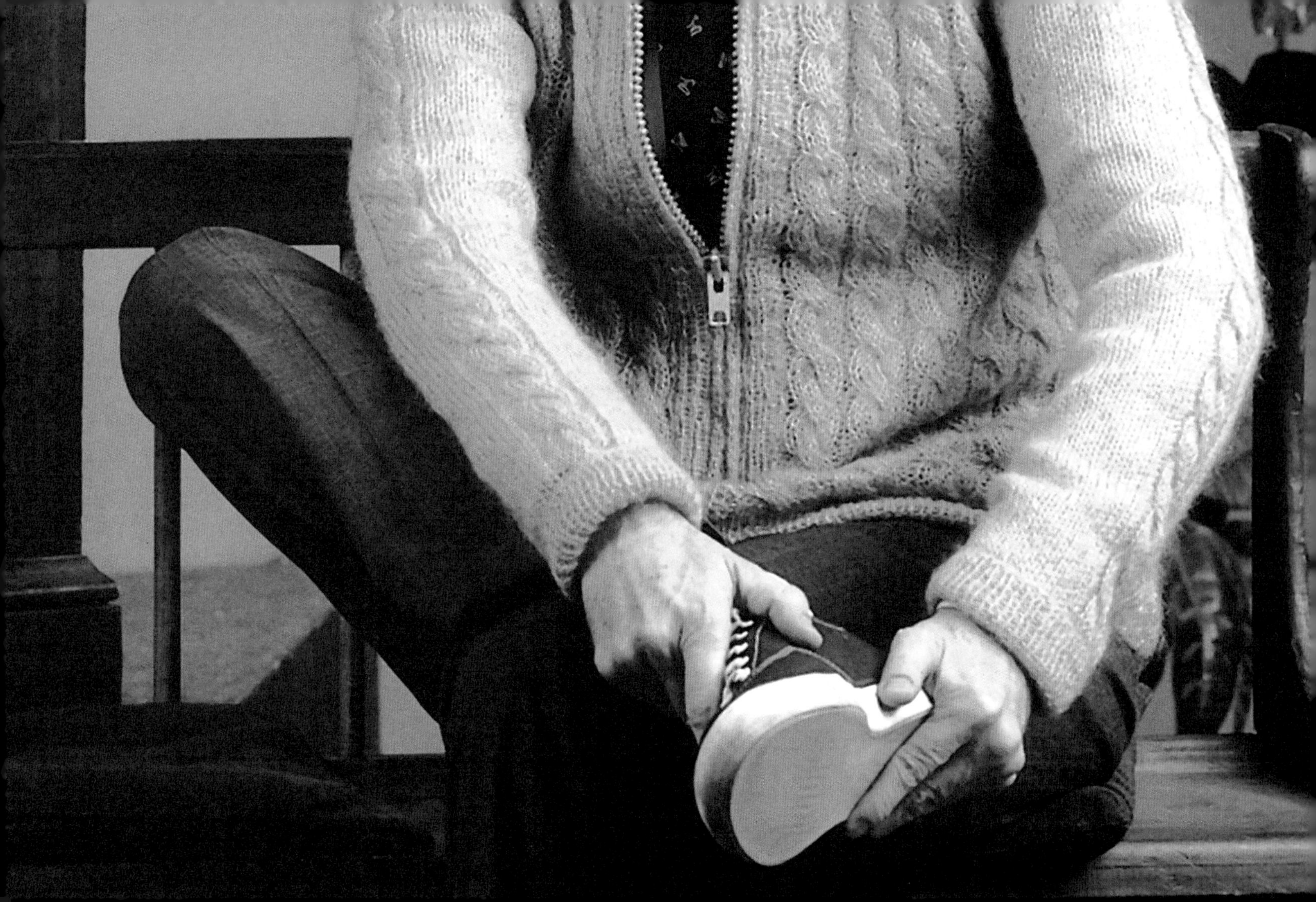

The communities of Southwestern Pennsylvania carry with them the same rubrics of facts and figures as any other locale— demographics that too often become the story when we look at a place. But the character sketch of a community can't be drawn in charts or graphs; the lyric beauty of a neighborhood can't be written with statistics.

Some Community Connections projects celebrated the poetic moments that make a community unique, whether in a single neighborhood, or the region as a whole. But to do so required imaginations that worked with equal poetry. Through film, drama, and community gatherings great and small, these projects prove that the Pittsburgh region is a place where symbols have strength: Where an image from a neighborhood, the words of a bygone era, or just a pair of sneakers and a sweater can conjure a new pride in the places we live.

WON'T YOU BE MY NEIGHBOR?
Ednan Alwan shakes his head — "no," he doesn't know who King Friday is, "But I know Mister Rogers." Five-year-old Ednan points to a TV showing episodes of the PBS favorite, "and I *know* Neighbor Land!" He may have the name wrong, but when it comes to the neighborhood — be it the Neighborhood of Make-Believe or *Mister Rogers' Neighborhood* — Ednan Alwan knows what he's talking about. In a way, he lives there.

On March 20, 2008, on what would have been his 80th birthday, all of Southwestern Pennsylvania came together to celebrate the legacy of Fred Rogers for the culmination of Won't You Be My Neighbor? Days — a week-long series of events organized by Family Communications, Inc., and supported by a Regional Grant. It's hard to imagine Rogers' legacy being fulfilled more emphatically than in the converted apartment in Pittsburgh's Prospect Park neighborhood, where Ednan and a dozen other children from this immigrant-heavy part of town had gathered.

The apartment acts as an integrated neighborhood base for the Greater Pittsburgh Literacy Council's Family Literacy Program. It was here that Ednan's mother, Hakima, learned English when she emigrated from Morocco eight years ago. Now she works for the Literacy Council, watching the kids as other parents — many of them political refugees from Burma, Burundi, and other far-flung locales — take English lessons. On Rogers' birthday, the apartment was packed with kids and their parents; food, games, and — of course — a TV showing episode after episode of *Mister Rogers* to an audience of rapt viewers.

Won't You Be My Neighbor? Days had many components: the groundbreaking for a new Fred Rogers statue on Pittsburgh's North Shore, big birthday bashes at the city's North Side museums and smaller ones in Rogers' hometown of Latrobe. There, local librarians quietly donned Fred's signature sweaters and sneakers as part of a worldwide Sweater Day — an effort to recognize Fred Rogers' achievements through the symbols he made his own — with sweater drives for the needy, open houses, and more.

Since Fred Rogers' passing in February, 2003, the Children's Museum of Pittsburgh has paid tribute to the city's favorite neighbor by opening its doors for free on his birthday. To celebrate Pittsburgh 250, Family Communications saw

Won't You Be My Neighbor? Days,
National Aviary, Pittsburgh

the opportunity to widen that effort to a region-wide event commemorating Mister Rogers' legacy of inclusivity.

Viewed from the cold perspective of statistics, Neighbor Days was obviously successful in its attempt to get families out to the region's wonderful amenities in order to bring Pittsburghers together. The Children's Museum recorded that 2,450 children visited that day — one of the best-attended days of their 25-year existence — and the story was the same at more than 70 other participating organizations and venues across the region. Project partner Tickets for Kids provided 450 free tickets to children for further events, and 5,000 books were distributed to kids from regional libraries.

But even though Fred Rogers knew his program reached thousands of kids, he always imagined neighborhoods built by approaching one kid at a time, and making sure they understood, "You are special." According to Margy Whitmer, a longtime producer of *Mister Rogers' Neighborhood* at Family Communications, the kind of small-scale event at Prospect Park might've been closest to Rogers' legacy.

"A lot of people who grew up watching the show, have kids who watch it now, and they finally get why they liked it so much," says Whitmer. "Kids need someone that makes them believe, 'he's talking to me.' They need a one-to-one feeling; that empathy."

Through components both large and small, Neighbor Days brought the people of Pittsburgh together, and made that kind of empathy just a little more possible. What seems most important is a child like Ednan Alwan seeing himself a little bit closer — to his mother, his neighborhood, his city and his region.

"That's what we hoped for," says Whitmer, "that, through this project, people would become more connected to their neighbors in positive ways. That's what Fred was always about — relationships."

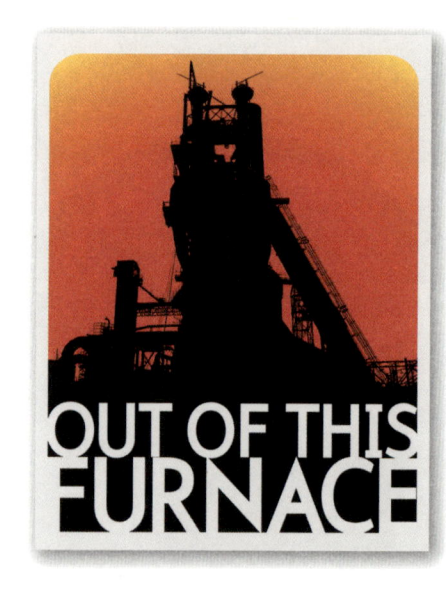

FORGING ALLIANCES

In the long-dormant dramatic adaptation of *Out of this Furnace*, Thomas Bell's classic novel of immigration and labor in turn-of-the-last-century Braddock, Allegheny County, prejudice against Eastern European mill workers is part of everyday life. That's a history most Pittsburghers know well. But the immigrant experience in Pittsburgh continues to be a vital part of the region's ongoing history—just look at Ednan and Hakima Alwan, and their neighbors in Prospect Park.

In addition to producing a revival of *Out of this Furnace* for Pittsburgh 250, with the help of a Grassroots Grant, Unseam'd Shakespeare Company examined immigrant labor and discrimination as continuing issues—not just pieces of history. To do so the Company commissioned two new plays: Wali Jamal's *Braddock 76*, about the African-American experience in 1970s Braddock, and Anya Martin's *Teatro Latino de Pittsburgh*, about the contemporary Latino immigrant experience in the region.

The tale of *Braddock 76* is a Shakespearean juxtaposition of a young, black, motherless boy falling in love with a young, Slavic, fatherless girl. The twist? Each one's parent is running for mayor of Braddock: he to be the first black mayor, she to be the first woman—a rather familiar electoral scenario in 2008. This allowed playwright Jamal to explore issues central to '70s Braddock: race relations, gender inequality, and the role of labor unions. *Braddock 76* also draws from the collective memory of Braddock's residents as told in oral histories gathered by Jamal and Unseam'd Shakespeare.

Similarly, to create *Teatro Latino de Pittsburgh*, Martin engaged a group of Latino immigrant students from area high schools. Using contemporary theater techniques aimed at "teaching how to write theater, not just on the page, but in time and space," as Martin puts it, as well as oral histories and interviews with Latino immigrants, Martin discovered that today's immigration stories closely resemble the days of *Out of this Furnace*.

"The two stories don't just intersect, they're almost the same," says Martin. "People are still coming for the same reasons: For a better life for their families, and because most feel like they don't have a choice. People see this city as earnest, honest, and hard-working, and that's a big part of this community's traditions; blue-collar and family-oriented."

With the revival of *Out of this Furnace*, Director Marci Woodruff sought to keep the play relevant for today's theater crowd, and also to bring to the stage a performance that could lure newcomers to drama with a snapshot of their ancestors' world. And the Unseam'd Shakespeare Company succeeded at this goal beyond their dreams: Every performance, including the two weeknight staged readings, sold out.

The result was a different look at the city's identity through Pittsburgh's immigrant history, in what Woodruff saw as a profound opportunity for social change.

"I believe in the power of theater to change people," says Woodruff. "If you can make people think for an hour that they're poor if they're not, or black if they're white — you can begin to change minds."

RELIABLE NARRATOR

Pittsburgh's Strip District neighborhood is a kind of neutral ground — the market territory where, on a busy Saturday morning, the city's wealthy and famous walk side-by-side with tourists, ordinary Joe's, and the far-less-fortunate. It's where Steelers players, for example, mingle with fans, so it's no real surprise to see legendary wide receiver Louis Lipps dropping a dollar into the cup of a panhandler dressed head-to-toe in fur-trimmed black-and-gold: Steelers Santa. Nor is it a surprise when The Strip's long-standing "Flute Man" takes a break from busking to call out: "Louis Lipps with another touchdown!"

The difference is that Steelers Santa isn't actually a panhandler, but actor Tommy Lafitte, portraying Steelers Santa for producer (and long-time Strip District business owner) Ray Werner's short film "Tommy and Me," the tale of a homeless man's difficult, but ultimately precious role in this high-visibility neighborhood. The flautist's shouts just go to prove that Werner and director Gregory Lehane have got every quirky detail of this neighborhood down pat.

And that's the key to *Greetings from Pittsburgh: Neighborhood Narratives*, the omnibus feature-film project, supported by a Grassroots Grant, of which "Tommy and Me" is but one part: nine films that each exemplify a specific Pittsburgh neighborhood.

In many ways, those neighborhoods reflect the same kind of uniqueness that the region's small towns do. And just as Community Connections sought to highlight the region by networking those disparate places, *Neighborhood Narratives* shows that — once brought together — these unique stories combine to say something about Pittsburgh.

"Each individual film expresses what it really means to be in that particular neighborhood," says *Neighborhood Narratives* project co-coordinator Kristen Lauth Shaeffer. "Pittsburghers have so much pride in their individual neighborhood identity and experience, and that's something we wanted to really capture."

In 2007, Shaeffer and Andrew Halasz were both students finishing MFA degrees in film at Chatham College. It was when discussing the recent omnibus feature *Paris J'Taime* — for which a group of famed directors created short pieces about Paris neighborhoods — that they realized that Pittsburgh could be seen through a similar lens.

"Something that really stands out about Pittsburgh is that all of the neighborhoods have a unique identity," says Shaeffer. "So we thought Pittsburgh would be an ideal location for a project like *Paris J'Taime*. And because it was Pittsburgh 250 — the timing just worked perfectly."

Production still from "Tommy and Me"

Carnegie Library of Homestead, Allegheny County

The pair assembled an advisory committee of local film-world icons—*Lightning Over Braddock* filmmaker Tony Buba, *The Bread, My Sweet* director Melissa Martin, and Women in Film and Media Executive Director Faith Dickinson—and began soliciting treatments. In seeking films about specific neighborhoods, the obvious route might have been documentaries, but the project leaders made an early decision to stick entirely to fictional narrative films.

Like in Gabrielle Reznek and Sam Turich's "Mombies," an uproarious satire of the gentrification of Lawrenceville by grown-up hipsters, which looks at the phenomenon of Pittsburgh's new family-oriented artsy crowd through the region's most famous film tradition: zombie flicks. Or, as in "Milk Crate," John Rice's film about a lifelong South Side resident whose neighbor—a young Japanese man and recent South Side transplant—makes the cultural faux pas of moving the crate used to mark the South Sider's parking space.

"How do you capture that in a documentary film?" says Shaeffer. "But John is a South Sider, and he's written about that unspoken understanding, and being the person coming in who doesn't know the rules."

Other films in *Neighborhood Narratives* include Tim Hall's film about the Hill District—comprised entirely of still photographs—and Jenn Golling and Matthew Fridg's story of a long-subdued love discovered in Homestead's library. In the sequence's last film, called simply "Regent Square," Nelson Chipman and Jeremy Braverman place a transplanted New Yorker in the eponymous neighborhood and expose him to neighborly traditions like welcome baskets and front-porch happy hours—much to his chagrin.

Neighborhood Narratives' debut screening at Pittsburgh Filmmakers' Regent Square Theater sold out in advance, and the project never looked back: Each of eight subsequent screenings, in the other eight represented neighborhoods, also sold out, calling for an encore run of five further screenings during the holidays.

Those neighborhood screenings—and the collaborations with community spaces and organizations that made them happen—marked one of the most important aspects of *Neighborhood Narratives*: That each film shows the indelible mark of its neighborhood, but also speak to the city's identity as a whole.

"These films aren't connected in terms of character, or story," says Shaeffer. "But together, the project forms a tapestry of the city—a feature film that tells what it means to live in Pittsburgh."

Chris Ivey, Filmmaker

**Liberty
for All**

Filmmaker Chris Ivey didn't expect things to be easy when he set out to make *East of Liberty: A Story of Good Intentions*, a multi-part documentary film about issues of race, class and gentrification resulting from the ongoing redevelopment of Pittsburgh's East Liberty neighborhood. But after finishing and screening its first part, Ivey ran into an unusual problem: His target audience—the people most affected by, or frustrated with, the situation—wasn't getting involved, or even attending the screenings.

"Of the 2,700 who came to the regular screenings, probably less than 500 were black—and that's the target audience! So, if they're not going to come out, I'm going to go to them."

In the summer of 2008, Ivey organized a series of free, outdoor screenings, supported by a Grassroots Grant, in traditionally African-American neighborhoods of Pittsburgh such as Homewood and the Hill District.

Expanding the film's audience wasn't Ivey's only motive. While making the film, "it was really a struggle, getting people to open up," says Ivey. "Any kind of media, in their opinion, always makes you look bad." The screenings provided Ivey with an opportunity to show those communities that he was telling the whole story, which he'll continue to do as a filmmaker as long as he's in Pittsburgh.

"There are some happy stories, some good things that happened, but of course some people make it, and some people don't," says Ivey. "A lot of people fall through the cracks, and we see some really sad stories, too.

"This is frank stuff, and I know it's frustrating for some local media to cover these communities. But, for one thing, just because I'm black, it's easier for me to get access to those communities—because I *am* them, so I have a real opportunity. It's all about telling the truth, about getting past that Pittsburgh politeness, and getting people to open up."

06: **PATHWAYS**

WE'RE NOT ONLY MAKING CLEANER WATER HERE, WE'RE CREATING A NEW ENVIRONMENT, A WETLANDS THAT'S TEEMING WITH LIFE.

Access. Appreciation. Conservation.

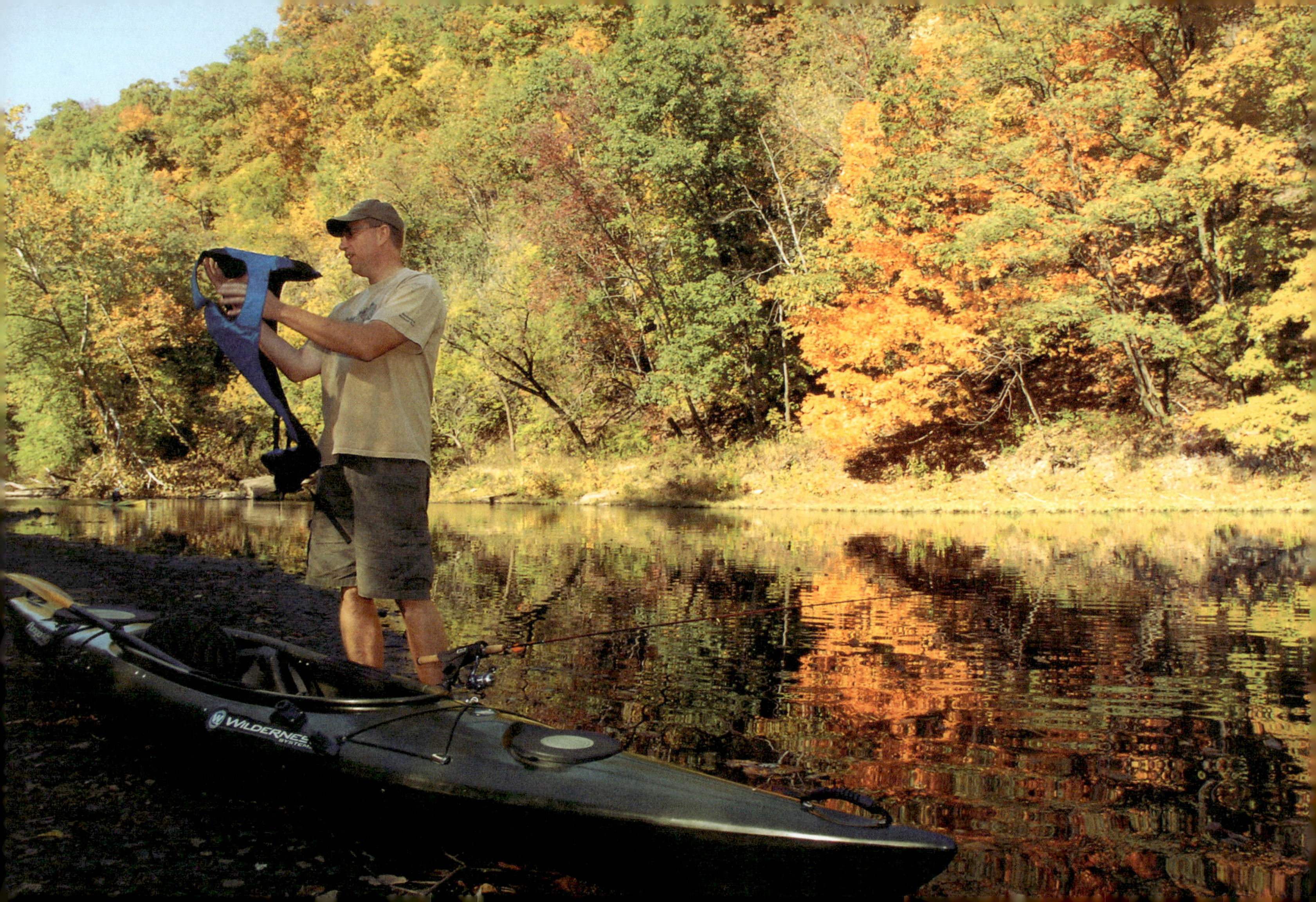

No: **03**\100 **Explore Western Pennsylvania's Wild Waterways** Awarded: $50,000

One of the long-standing ironies of Pittsburgh's reputation is that, despite being known for so long as the smoky Steel City, one can travel a few miles in almost any direction out of the city's center and escape into an idyllic countryside unlike that surrounding almost any other metropolitan area. This irony, however, is one that Western Pennsylvanians cherish: Those trails, waterways, ponds and fields are as much a part of the region's identity as its industrial heritage or deep-rooted history.

As a part of Community Connections, many projects cut paths to increase the understanding of, and access to, the region's outdoor amenities, be that miles outside of town or just around the corner. Because the depth of this region's environmental beauty is something that Pittsburgh—perhaps because of its decades with smoke-darkened skies—never takes for granted.

FISHERMEN OF MEN

Sitting on the shore, Rodney Bryant points east, away from the boathouse and towards the deepest part of the lake in North Park, Allegheny County. That's where he used to catch catfish and trout on his weekly trips to the park, he explains, "until I had my first heart attack, three years ago. I haven't been here since. Not 'til today."

Bryant's most recent trip to North Park, on a made-to-order sunny summer's afternoon, wasn't necessarily about catching fish. With Fisherman's Tale, a Grassroots Project lead by the century-old senior-care organization Lemington Community Services (LCS), Bryant and over a dozen other African-American seniors—largely from the Lincoln-Lemington neighborhood of Pittsburgh—visited North Park to catch some rays, catch up with friends, and tell some stories. And if those stories happened to reflect on the state of their mental and physical health, LCS Executive Director Joy Starzl says, all the better.

"We've always had a guy's night at the center, where the seniors come in and play cards and talk," says Starzl. "We bring someone in to talk about an issue, but not to stand up and talk about it—they just sit around and play cards with the guys, and bring up things like grieving and depression. But the men stopped coming, so we thought, we need to expose them to this information. We did a survey, and they said, 'we don't wanna play cards—we want to go fishing!'"

Fisherman's Tale brought the guy's night outside. Along with the seniors, LCS took a few extra folks along on their trips: Doctors, psychologists, neighbors and friends who could casually chat with the fishermen and find out what's really going on with them. Lincoln-Lemington, along with several other predominantly African-American neighborhoods in Pittsburgh from which LCS draws the majority of its clientele, is a rough place to be a senior citizen. A lack of amenities geared towards seniors, coupled with a high crime rate, tends to keep people isolated—which allows them to slip through the cracks too often. With the success of Fisherman's Tale, LCS project coordinator Arnold Perry hoped that the project would help to stem that decline.

"We try to bring together people who too-often stay in their homes," says Perry. "People need events like Fisherman's Tale so that they don't feel neglected and unwanted. Jesus told Peter to be a 'fisherman of men,' and that's what we try to be."

№: **20**\100   **Fisherman's Tale**   Awarded: $5,000

While the initial plan for the project was limited to senior citizens, the immediate appeal of Fisherman's Tale allowed it to blossom much further. Thanks to a separate grant from Mount Ararat Baptist Church, Fisherman's Tale began including children from Pittsburgh's Paulson Community Center in their trips later in the summer. The addition leant a new element to the project's title, allowing the seniors to tell their tales to a new generation of African-American youths.

"The kids that have come—I'm at a loss for words," says Starzl. "They come and they listen to the guys, and afterwards, they tell their friends about it and their friends want to go, too. They want to go again and again. And that's so important, because if we don't get these guys to tell their stories, they will regret it, and one day the kids will regret it, too."

RAPIDS ASCENT

When Frank Moone looks at the waterways that connect Southwestern Pennsylvania, it's not bass, trout, or walleye he imagines, but the rapids, eddies and calms sought by kayakers and canoeists. As a board member with the Wild Waterways Conservancy, Moone helped to spearhead the Explore Western Pennsylvania's Wild Waterways project, building boat launches for non-mechanized crafts throughout Beaver, Butler and Lawrence counties.

According to Moone, the Connoquenessing and Slippery Rock waterways offer a broad variety of paddling possibilities—from placid waters for the beginner to rapids for the experienced boater. The challenge for the conservancy has been to provide access to those waterways with minimal intrusion on the environment.

"Traditionally, boat launches are big concrete slab things that you back a truck onto," says Moone. "We're not interested in anything like that. Ours are made of native sandstone blocks, with steps or mulched trails, to carry a kayak down on. The idea is to encourage the use of the outdoors, but discourage improper use."

Over the summer and fall of 2008, Wild Waterways built four launches on the Connoquenessing Creek, and a further launch on Slippery Rock Creek. The result is a fully accessible yet environmentally sound water trail, which not only serves the people of Southwestern Pennsylvania, but makes a new destination for kayaking and canoeing enthusiasts from all over the country.

"The launches on the Connoquenessing cover the bulk of the Connie water trail," says Moone. "So now, if you're a beginner and want flat water, we've got a space for you—you won't have to paddle ten miles to get out of the water. But there's another stretch—from Ellwood City Gorge to Rock Point—that's serious Class 3 and Class 4 rapids, and it was hard to get in and out of the water there. This makes that available, and we expect a big influx of people; people who know what they're doing, and who like a challenge."

MINE CONTROL

Maybe it's the pastoral setting, or the heightened awareness to the outdoors that comes with a sun-dappled day, but on a bright morning, the colors near the intersection of Tanoma Road and Rayne Church Road seem raised like ridges. There's the dusty blacktop of Tanoma Road, the kind of rural Indiana County country lane that's as much part of the landscape as a forest or farm; the green glint of rain-slickened grass; and then there's the bed of the ravine—a rusty red more befitting Crayola than countryside.

"Anyone who grew up in the Pittsburgh area before about the mid-'80s, they know these colors," says Rebecca Slak, board member of the Evergreen Conservancy, pointing to a gusher of rust water spurting from the ground a hundred yards below—water pumped out by natural pressure from an abandoned mine deep below. The water's metallic tint is from the tons of iron it has absorbed from the mine, which then flows down into Crooked Creek—a tributary of the Allegheny. By the time the Allegheny River hits Kittanning, the iron has entered the entire region's water supply.

Or at least it would, but for a relatively simple, beautifully natural example of an Abandoned Mine Drainage treatment system. A quarter of a mile from the ravine sit three ponds, each almost unnoticeably lower than its predecessor, surrounded by streams and together creating a wetlands environment in the middle of coal country. With help from a Grassroots Grant, in the fall of 2008, the Evergreen Conservancy signposted a new trail around the Tanoma Wetlands, explaining its operations and its importance to the ecosystem of the region.

As visiting classes, Scout troops, and Sunday drivers can now discover for themselves, water contaminated and forced by natural pressure from the mine is directed into the first Wetlands pond, where iron sinks to the bottom—these tons of metals can be collected and recycled. As it slowly moves through the three ponds, the natural clumpings of Wetlands plants filter the water—the entire process is natural and simple, and requires almost no upkeep.

At the end of the third pond, the now-purified water trickles into a small stream that leads into Crooked Creek. As the new signage on the Tanoma Wetlands Educational Trail explains, the whole process not only makes the water safer for humans, it has allowed the local ecosystem to rebuild itself, and new life to flourish in this corner of Indiana County.

"This takes almost 150 pounds of iron out of Crooked Creek *per day*," says Tom Clark, an environmental scientist with the Susquehanna River Basin. "That's a whole person of iron every day. But we're not only making cleaner water here, we're creating a new environment, a wetlands that's teeming with life."

Pedestrian Crossing

Outside of Michael Edwards' stately house on Pittsburgh Street in Connellsville, Fayette County, a freestanding sign is posted, explaining the history of the block's grand homes. It's easy to see why Edwards and his partner moved here from Washington, D.C., seven years ago—the house is the kind of property that would command multiple millions of dollars in a bustling city's market. "We drove up one day from D.C. to take a look at it," says Edwards. "We didn't even stay the night," before deciding to move.

Edwards has since devoted most of his time to helping Connellsville emerge from a post-industrial slumber that's lasted decades, with initiatives like the Connellsville Cultural Trust and its Main Street Program. Through his most recent effort, the Connellsville Heritage Trail, a two-mile walking tour of the town including 11 informational signs at historic locations, Edwards hopes to attract other D.C.-to-Pittsburgh travelers—this time, though, they won't be coming in cars.

"Connellsville is the only sizeable place where the Great Allegheny Passage bike trail passes right through the town," says Edwards. "We want to get people off the trail, and walking into town."

The town of Waynesburg, in Greene County, considers itself to have once been the starting point for a historic trail of another sort. Pittsburgh and St. Louis may be more famous, but Waynesburg native Mary Beth Pastorius claims her hometown was the first launching pad for westward expansion.

"Greene County was really the road to the West," says Pastorius, a Waynesburg property owner and committed preservationist. "A lot of people in here are proud of their pioneer heritage, and there's a great historical understanding of the people. What we want to do is spread that to the buildings."

When 18th-century pioneer Thomas Slater bought the piece of land that would become Waynesburg, he referred to his plot as "Eden." That acreage has retained its historical foothold, and today Waynesburg offers fine examples of High Victorian Italianate, Georgian revival, and other 19th- and early-20th-century architectural styles. Over 600 Waynesburg structures—a third of all its properties—are on Pennsylvania's historic register.

"We want Waynesburg to be a destination," says Pastorius. "You can't be known for everything, so what's special about your town? For us, it's that streetscape."

With Rediscovering Eden: The Historic Waynesburg Walking Tour, local residents and visitors began to appreciate and understand the importance of this architecture. By walking, Pastorious believes Waynesburg residents can get reacquainted with their own neighborhood, and find a new sense of pride in their community's history.

It's a notion that's shared by Valentine Brkich when he talks about his Beaver County home.

"It used to be that, if you lived in Bridgewater, you walked to the store," says Brkich. "You talked to your neighbors on the porch, you passed by people on the street. You knew things about *your* community because you walked on *your* streets, in your town."

The memory of the way things used to be is ever-present in Brkich's life, whose family history is closely tied to his hometown. His grandfather served as mayor for nearly four decades and built the house that Brkich now lives in, the same house where his own father was born.

"I have a big interest in getting people to take pride in this community," says Brkich, "to recognize the treasures they have. So I wanted to take these river towns here in Beaver County, bring attention to them, and connect them."

Towards that goal, Brkich devised the River Town Community Walking Maps project, mapping pedestrian paths in each of ten communities along the Ohio and Beaver rivers. The walks combine the towns' downtown amenities and heritage sites, plus provide a brief historical overview.

While Brkich himself assembled the histories, choosing the walking routes and points of interest was a collaborative effort with the downtown-partnership organizations in each community—one of many links between river towns like Beaver, Rochester, Monaca, and Bridgewater.

"People don't walk anymore, and it's one of the things that has taken away the community aspect of our towns."

07: **RESPONSIBILITY**

IT MADE ME THINK — WHAT ABOUT PEOPLE WHO AREN'T LIKE ME, AND DON'T HAVE THE OPTIONS I HAVE?

Need. Give. Change.

JUST DO RIGHT   Genesis 4:7

Nº: **80**/100　**C3 Performance Car Care Ministry**　Awarded: $5,000

It's the oldest kind of community engagement: A loaf of bread, a bottle of medicine, protection from harm, a helping hand extended to a neighbor in their time of need. In the town halls, churches, nonprofit offices, and living rooms of Southwestern Pennsylvania, helping to serve the basic needs of one's neighbor isn't an extraordinary event tied to an anniversary or region-wide initiative, but a part of everyday life.

So when Community Connections gathered people from around the region to imagine the ways they could enhance their communities, it was no surprise that a host of engaging and creative ideas evolved that would help the underserved. But in economically troubled areas of Mercer County, the Mon Valley, the City of Pittsburgh and more, Community Connections projects not only helped to serve those in need, they brought our region just a little bit closer together—and brought a few more helping hands within reach.

TRANSIT AUTHORITY
Their hands covered in grease, their backs bent, hunched over a car's engine—Pastor Phil Beck and Josh Salley of Central Community Church (C3 for short) in Transfer, Mercer County, have a funny word for what they do in a cramped garage each Friday night: ministry. It's an expression of faith encapsulated by the slogan on the back of their T-shirts—"Just Do Good"— and one that Beck subscribes to whole-heartedly.

"I want to get out of what I call 'the holy huddle,'" says Beck. "We've got to stop talking about the playbook, and get out there and run the plays!"

Across Route 18 from the Central Community Church in Transfer sits a former strip mall, donated for the church's use. In one corner of the building, fellow Michigan-to-Mercer transplants Beck and Salley—the two car enthusiasts arrived separately and met serendipitously—operate the C3 Performance Car Care Ministry.

Every Friday night, locals with lots of car trouble but little money can get free-to-cheap oil changes, assessments, and minor repair work as part of Central Community Church's mission of ceaseless community service. With help from a Grassroots Grant, the Church was able to renovate a garage-like space within the old mall and begin to process the stack of applications they received for help with auto repair. The

Josh Salley, C3 Performance Car Care Ministry mechanic

Church acquired donated parts and help from several local garages, and a lot of loving labor from Beck's parishioners—all of the hours put into renovating the space were volunteered. And while a church-operated car mechanic might seem strange to some, in Mercer County, it just makes sense.

The sparsely populated territories of Mercer County, 65 miles north of Pittsburgh, are caught in something of a no-man's-land. Mercer's a little too far south for Erie's orbit, and that pesky border keeps it from latching onto Youngstown, Ohio—even though its proximity to that city ironically designates Mercer as an "urban" area in the eyes of many federal agencies. With a widespread population, and little-to-no public transit available between most of its towns, just getting from place to place becomes the number one issue.

Most descriptions of Southwestern Pennsylvania, omit Mercer County, too. So when the opportunity arose to participate in Community Connections, with its expanded view of the Pittsburgh region, projects in Mercer County turned out in numbers. And, unsurprisingly, many directly addressed that transportation issue.

"Transportation is the big problem here," says Michael Wright, president and CEO of the Shenango Valley Urban League, and a Grassroots decisionmaker for Mercer County. "If you don't have your own vehicle, you can't get a job, you can't even go to the doctor—you can't do anything."

For some Mercer County residents, getting from Hermitage to Sharon isn't an option, never mind a trip to Pittsburgh, even if one's physical or mental health depends on it. That's why the Community Counseling Center of Mercer County came up with the idea for its Telepsychiatry Project—a program to help provide access to psychiatric medical help for Mercer County kids without their families having to make the trip to Pittsburgh.

"Because we're in this in-between area, there are a lot of services that we don't have much access to—including mental health professionals," says Fern Torok, Community Counseling's community outreach and development coordinator. "But we do have an affiliation with Western Psychiatric Institute and Clinic in Pittsburgh. There are a *lot* of doctors available there—and a lot of kids up here who need their help. We're trying to address the distance issue, and Western Psych already had a telepsychiatry program: it was up and running, we knew it worked."

In telepsychiatry, patients can have their initial visits with a certified psychiatrist over a computer-based long-distance video and audio system. Patients—in this case primarily children—can receive diagnosis, and in some cases even prescriptions, over the system, without having to physically visit the doctor.

"I always wish there was no reason for us to have a job," says Torok. "But there is a real need, and with a program like this, we're able to provide better access to services, sooner, and get kids started earlier with the attention they need."

HOME PLATE

For the Westmoreland County Food Bank, Greensburg is something of a riddle: The county's seat and largest city, only eight miles south of the Food Bank's Delmont headquarters, and yet frequently out of reach.

"Greensburg is hugely important for us," says Deana Pastor, program director for Westmoreland County Food Bank. "And before our Community Connections grant, our Operation Fresh Express program hadn't been there for two years because we didn't have a sponsor."

Operation Fresh Express takes fresh and perishable foods into the county's various communities, using two refrigerated trucks, to supplement the non-perishable items that the Food Bank's "food box" recipients receive monthly. On average, community visits service 150–200 people per trip, all with donated food—the program began in 1999 as a way to distribute the perishable items received at regular donation points before they had to be thrown out. During the summer months, Operation Fresh Express also receives donations from local farmers' "hunger garden" crops designated for Food Bank donation.

Operation Fresh Express requires volunteers and donated goods to work, both of which it had. But it still costs money, even just to run the trucks—about $350 per trip, which must be donated by a community sponsor. With a Grassroots Grant, the Food Bank was able to jumpstart and standardize the Operation Fresh Express schedule, thereby building its capacity to reach more people more frequently.

By using their grant money to revisit areas like Greensburg and Monessen that Operation Fresh Express had been missing, the program raised its visibility and was able to woo enough new sponsors to fill its calendar for 2009 in advance. In the Mount Pleasant area, which hadn't received regular visits in years, the Food Bank was able to solicit 2009 sponsorship by inviting a potential sponsor to volunteer at a grant-funded 2008 Operation Fresh Express visit.

"This program always operates at a deficit," says Pastor. "That's OK—we don't want to throw away good food just because it'll expire. But we have to have a sponsor to make it work. There are a few regular sponsors—churches, rotary clubs—but other than those communities, service is hit-and-miss. That's why the grant was so important—it got us back into these communities."

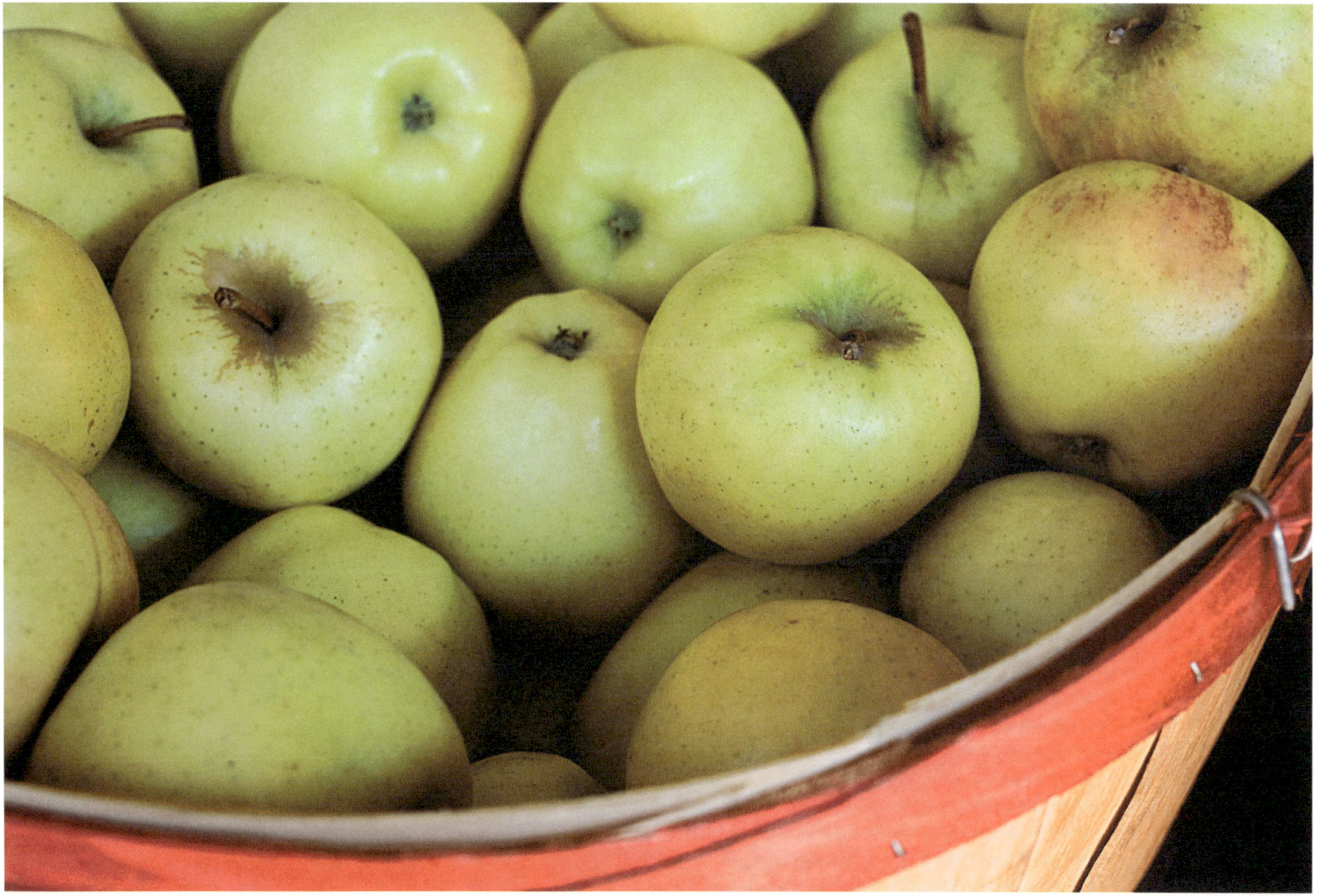

Nº: **71**\100 Main Street Classic 5K Run/Walk for the Homeless   Awarded: $5,000

Gritty concentration and joyful determination: The faces of the runners who turned out in force for Fayette County's Main Street Classic 5K Run/Walk for the Homeless reveal a desire to succeed, and a knowledge that they're running for a reason. Hosted by Uniontown's homeless-aid organization, City Mission-Living Stones, the Main Street Classic gave participants a chance to come together on a beautiful summer's day to raise awareness for less fortunate members of the community. The Main Street Classic wasn't about running away from the region's problems, but about neighbors uniting to confront those problems, head on and at full speed.

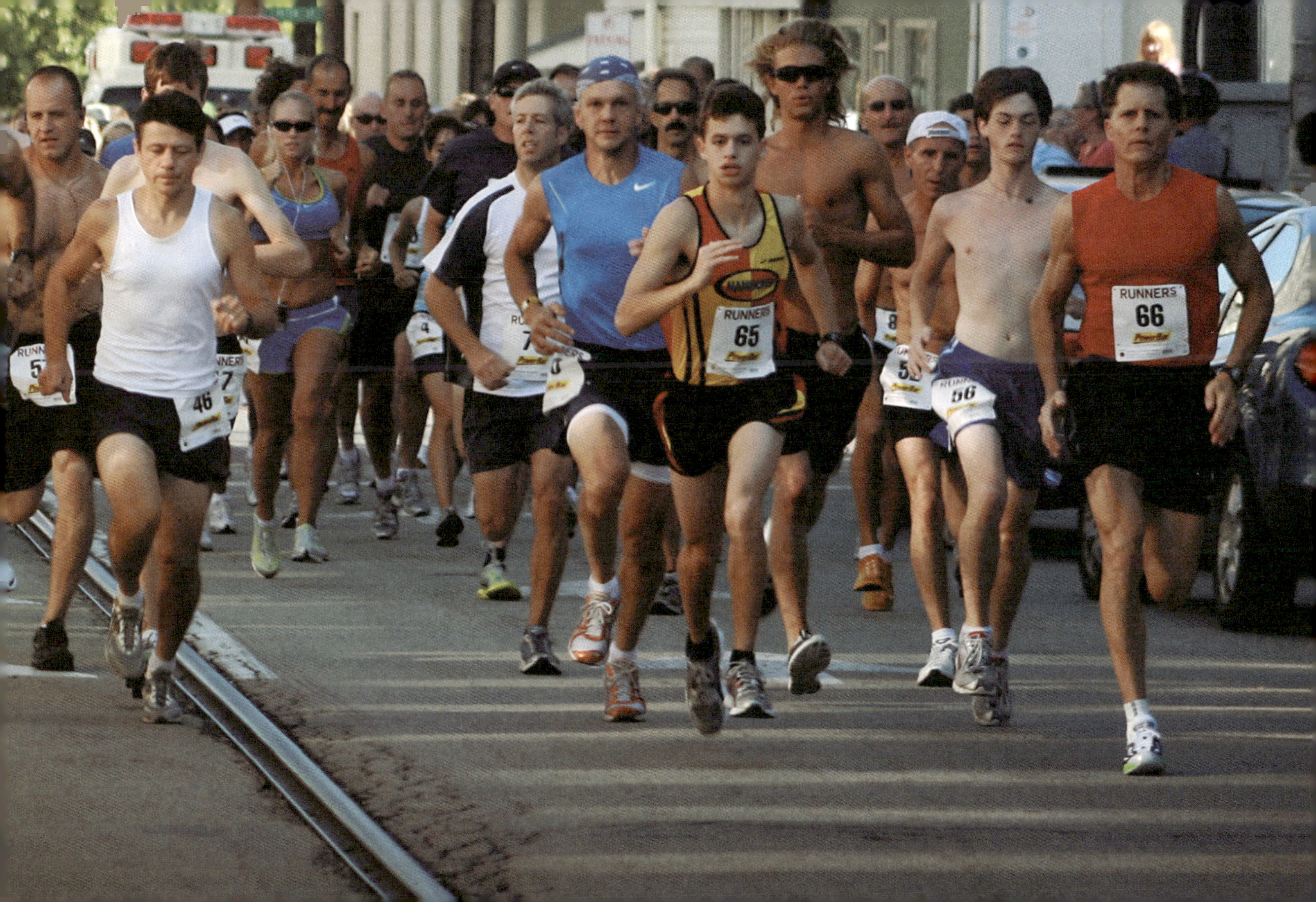
RUNNERS
66
RUNNERS
65
RUNNERS
56
46

Jude Vachon, Project Manager

Information Prescription

When Jude Vachon injured her shoulder in 2005, she could hardly have imagined that it would be the catalyst that led her life in an entirely new direction. Vachon had good reason to believe that, although uninsured at the time, she would be able to find whatever assistance was available to help cover medical expenses. After all, Vachon had experience as an educator and community activist, and was well on her way to her current career as a librarian in Pittsburgh's Carnegie Public Library system. If there was information out there, she'd be able to find it.

"But it was all extremely difficult," says Vachon. "It was hard for me to find any help, and I'm a big information geek! It made me think—what about people who aren't like me, and don't have the options I have? No internet access, no personal connections—it just hit me how in the dark people are without information."

In the aftermath of her own problems, Vachon began writing things down—the addresses and phone numbers, names and notes that can help to navigate the maze of organizations and programs that exist in the Pittsburgh area to help the medically uninsured. Under the simple name Be Well!, Vachon began publishing a booklet of all that information, distributing it to one of the least-insured demographics—18- to 40-year-olds.

Be Well! was immediately successful, running through 6,000 copies and about 10 separate revisions as it garnered more attention and built relationships with healthcare providers and organizations around Pittsburgh. But Vachon realized that the audience she was reaching wasn't necessarily the one that needed this help the most: The uninsured are represented with wildly disproportionate numbers in African-American communities, particularly amongst seniors. So, Vachon received a Grassroots Grant to build upon Be Well!'s relationship with St. Andrew's Lutheran Church, within reach of multiple target neighborhoods like East Liberty and the Hill District, and expand the project's impact with a new print run of the Be Well! booklet.

Through information sessions and community health fairs at St. Andrew's, Be Well! provided everything from traditional medical services—free blood-pressure checks and HIV screenings—to introductions to non-mainstream health options, such as doula and midwife birthing programs. But Vachon says that the real breakthrough came not necessarily from meetings and sessions, but from old-fashioned legwork.

"Sometimes people see that there's a healthcare fair and have this sense that, 'there's nothing there for me,'" says Vachon. "You have to go to where people really are. We took booklets to corner stores and braiding salons, putting fliers up on telephone polls—everything. Access to information has to come first, and that means I've got to try to be as far-reaching as possible."

08: **PERCEPTIONS**

THIS REGION IS PERFECT FOR DISCUSSING THE PROCESS THROUGH WHICH WE CONSTRUCT THE IDEA OF A PLACE. WE WANT PEOPLE TO TAKE A CLOSER LOOK AT THE ENVIRONMENT THAT SURROUNDS THEM.

People. Places. Creativity.

WILTSHIRE MOTEL

The complexities of meaning in contemporary art make strange bedfellows indeed: A billboard seen from the highway and a piece of music arranged for brass band; paintings hung in bus shelters and in nooks and crannies of a do-it-yourself gallery space. Taken out of context, these disparate works might seem as unrelated as could be. But contemporary art is *about* context—about the curator as artist—and, in the right hands, such works can be arranged into a new whole, describing a new way of looking at the world.

TWIN HI-WAY DRIVE-IN

AARKE T
N O Y

As a part of Community Connections, a handful of artistic endeavors used a wide array of media to build new ways to perceive our communities. Whether that was a vision of the built environment Southwestern Pennsylvanians inhabit, a theme to act as soundtrack for the city, or a bold imagining of the region's artistic abundance, those projects worked toward a common goal: To offer a new perception of the Pittsburgh region's artistic past and future, by offering a different glimpse of its creative present.

SIGNS OF THE TIMES

The tilt of a Tiki-like neon "T." The star that dots an "i," somewhere between a cartoon and a Christmas-tree ornament. The pastel aquas and pinks that color in those letters, like a ghost of Miami on Steubenville Pike.

The simplicity and fragility of a sign, like the Twin Hi-Way Drive-In Theatre's classic sign in Robinson Township, can be both its greatest beauty and its kiss of death: Why keep something built for a function after that function has passed? But to the founders and participants of the Pittsburgh Signs Project, that simplicity holds a beauty worth savoring; that fragility, something worth holding onto.

Since 2004, Jennifer Baron, Greg Langel, Elizabeth Perry, and Mark Stroup have captured images of the signage that dots Southwestern Pennsylvania's landscapes, and shared them with the world on their celebrated website, www.pittsburghsigns.org. And with the book *Pittsburgh Signs Project: 250 Signs of Western Pennsylvania*, funded by a Regional Grant, the project took a significant step forward.

Since its inception, Pittsburgh Signs Project has been, according to Stroup, a way of examining and celebrating the objects that comprise our places—just as we examine and celebrate the cultural affectations that we, as people, are comprised of. For *250 Signs of Western Pennsylvania*, the project brought those two elements together, with a region-wide call for photographers both amateur and professional; dozens of photographers, from all 14 Southwestern Pennsylvania counties, contributed photos of signs to the book. And in doing so, created a compendium of regional lore.

Some of the included signs are obvious choices. Others, far less so: A farm's sign, made of tires, or handwritten roadside notes on rural roads.

"We hope that this project can push the conversation about Pittsburgh as a place," says Stroup. "This region is perfect for discussing the process through which we construct the *idea* of a place—the mythology that informs our view of the place we live. We want people to take a closer look at the environment that surrounds them."

Pittsburgh Signs Project has done that in a number of ways besides its online presence, from walks around various sign-heavy locations, to shows of photographs at galleries and group events. With *250 Signs*, an entire new audience has opened up for the project: With heavy local and national publicity, including an Associated Press story, that conversation about Pittsburgh has gone from web phenomenon to the recognition reserved for more durable objects.

For Jennifer Baron, removing the project from its web-based environment only heightens its power. Through the team's relationship with Carnegie Mellon University's STUDIO for Creative Inquiry, The Carnegie Mellon University Press agreed to act as publisher—with the added benefit of a nationwide distribution through Cornell University Press.

"The book is about capturing and documenting this aspect of our visual culture in a tangible way, and then giving it room to breathe," says Baron. "You can have a personal experience with this, and then go on the website and talk with everyone around the world about it."

But, *250 Signs* is, at its heart, about uniting a region to look at one aspect of a shared landscape. That's a goal that's reached by both the project's contributors—from professional photographers, to college kids, rank amateurs, and in one case, an autistic teenager—and by its medium: the thoughtfulness that goes into building something tangible and permanent.

"You never look at the world in that way," says Baron, "where you just pick apart one little thing over and over. Our culture is always about millions of things, all going at once. But there's something poetic about just looking at one little thing."

ACADEMY REWARDS

At dusk on a hot summer's evening in Pittsburgh, August Wilson peered through the window of a bus shelter. Not the man, of course, nor even a photograph, but rather local artist Tom Mosser's impressionistic portrait of the famed playwright, "The Eyes of August."

And somehow, Wilson's brightly colored gaze changed everything: The quality of the light; the rich swirl of heated haze in the air; the Hopper-esque composition of a street-corner moment. Viewed in this new context, thanks to Mosser's painting, this ordinary Pittsburgh moment became a living urban artwork.

To place fine artwork within the community—to make it not an imposition, but an integrated part of ordinary peoples' daily lives—is a goal we can imagine Wilson would've approved of. And it was a goal that the community-operated art school The Academy of the South Side achieved with *Citywide Salon*, a month-long show of local artwork in city bus shelters, supported by a Grassroots Grant.

The idea came in a flash. Artist Tim Meehan saw a vulgar radio-station ad posted inside a shelter like the ones he and fellow Academy co-founder Dan Vogel waited in every day. "It was so tacky," says Meehan, "I just thought, 'why can't there be something beautiful in there?'" And for the month of June 2008, there was. During *Citywide Salon*, local artists displayed their work in Port Authority Transit bus shelters spanning

№: **16**\100   Citywide Salon   Awarded: $5,000

Pittsburgh neighborhoods from the South Side to Bloomfield, Oakland to East Liberty, and many in between; temporarily redrawing the city's map with artists rather than intersections, and changing the way people saw their town.

At the downtown intersection of Cherry Way and Boulevard of the Allies, Cory Bonnet's cityscape, "Gold Light: Pittsburgh," was like an introduction or a handshake. Its haze of hues and light lies somewhere between that of an optimistic summer's morning, and the thick fug of history that hangs just out of reach in the city's air. Across the street from that location sits the Art Institute of Pittsburgh, where Vogel and Meehan first struck on the idea for The Academy of the South Side.

"We thought, 'what if there was something for contemporary realist painting like the Art Institute is for graphic design?'" Vogel recalled.

Less than a year later, The Academy of the South Side opened, offering classes and live-model sessions to anyone interested in drawing and painting technique and theory, taught by local artists at the Brew House art space in the South Side.

When The Academy purchased a bus shelter ad on the South Side's Carson Street to announce their classes a few years back, it opened their eyes to the possibilities of this citywide canvas: At less than $300 for a month-long rental, including the creation of a shelter-wall-sized poster of their artwork, Vogel and Meehan realized how easily one could parlay a small grant into a citywide salon.

With enough funding secured, the Academy began accepting submissions and chose 19 high-visibility bus stops, and an equal number of artists from over 80 submissions. The result was the kind of subtle artistic imposition achieved by "The Eyes of August" on its landscape. But the project's legacy may prove to be a constant swirl of such work. Now that the precedent is set, Vogel and Meehan say the possibilities seem endless.

"We're trying to take 'fine art' into the street," says Vogel. "We want to show people, this kind of realist painting isn't just gallery art. So I suppose that the medium is actually in the Warholian tradition—it's pop, even if the artwork itself isn't."

PORTRAITS IN BRASS AND STEEL

When the River City Brass Band decided to highlight the music of the many world-famous musicians that hail from the Pittsburgh region, the nationally-regarded concert band found a lot to choose from. There are famed singers and players like Dakota Staton and George Benson. And then there are composers like the legendary Henry Mancini and Billy Strayhorn—and a few new composers like Carson Cooman and Marilyn Taft-Thomas who, one day, just might become legends themselves.

While it would've been easy for the Band just to cull the repertoires of over a century of Pittsburgh musicians and composers in celebration of Pittsburgh 250, the region's long-standing vanguard of smart, fun concert music made a bold decision: To commission seven brand-new pieces of music

№: **01**\100 Celebrate Pittsburgh: River City Brass Band Music Commissioning Project   Awarded: $50,000

from composers with regional connections, based on their visions of Pittsburgh. As the Band's music director and conductor, Denis Colwell knew as well as anyone that debuting a new piece of music is a risky proposition—but that the rewards can be just as great.

"There's never a guarantee that the audience is going to like a new piece, of course," says Colwell. "But we try to keep a balance on our programs—of the old and the new. With enough new arrangements of old favorites to sink their teeth into, I like to believe an audience will grant you the opportunity to try something brand new. After all, every piece of music was a debut at some point!"

For their Celebrate Pittsburgh project, the River City Brass Band commissioned and debuted new pieces such as "Portrait in Brass and Steel" by Mike Tomaro, a Band member and head of Jazz Studies at Duquesne University; recent musical composition graduate Carson Cooman's "Pittsburgh Rhapsody"; and "Snapshots of a Great City" by former dean of Carnegie Mellon's music school, Marilyn Taft-Thomas.

While debuting new music was the most ambitious part of River City Brass Band's project, it would never have been enough for this hard-working ensemble to expose the music only to a Downtown Pittsburgh audience. As part of its mission to maintain an expanded focus and bring music to the region, rather than forcing the region to come to them, the Band's 2008 calendar saw the band perform each of its programs in at least seven locations—from Westmoreland to Cambria to Beaver counties, and all over Allegheny County.

To Colwell, the next step for these commissioned compositions is to see to their addition to, and survival in, the popular repertoire, which means reaching out beyond the brass band world.

"There are only two professional brass bands in the U.S.," says Colwell. "So the number of performances likely is very limited. All too often, a piece gets written and premiered, and that's it. But once you transcribe these pieces for concert band, there are hundreds of options—every school in the country has one."

With a host of talented arrangers within the Band's ranks, including composers such as Tomaro, making those transcriptions a reality won't be difficult—allowing the music from Celebrate Pittsburgh to remain in circulation for years to come.

YEAR BOOK

Jill Larson knew exactly what she wanted *In The Making: 250 Years/250 Artists* to accomplish, and the five-month long exhibition at Fe gallery in Pittsburgh's Lawrenceville neighborhood certainly hit its mark. While many small, independent gallery shows might go for stylistic cohesion, minimalist organization, or conceptual interdependence, Larson wanted *In The Making* to inspire a radically different emotion.

"I wanted people to be overwhelmed," says Larson, Fe gallery's volunteer artistic director. "I wanted them to have the same impression I had when I moved here—to take a step back, right when they walk in, and have that experience I had."

That experience was an age-old Pittsburgh story: Drawn to the city for reasons beyond her control, an artist discovers that, rather than a smoggy culture-free zone, Pittsburgh boasts a thriving arts scene comparable to much larger cities. Upon arriving from Atlanta, Larson was initially overwhelmed, and immediately wanted to tell the world about the wealth of talent in her new home.

"I was *shocked* to find how many good artists were living in this region," says Larson. "I was shocked by the quantity and the quality of the work being done here, and I really wanted to show other people!"

Larson quickly organized an exhibit connecting Atlanta and Pittsburgh artists, which showed in both cities, including what was meant to be a one-time use of space that Fe gallery (named for the periodic-table symbol for iron) now inhabits. After more than five years, Fe—now a nonprofit organization and volunteer-staffed gallery—is still thriving.

When the opportunity to celebrate Pittsburgh's 250th arose, Larson conceived of a new way to broadcast the region's depth of artistic talent: 250 artists, drawn from all 14 counties of the region, crowded together on Fe's walls, creating a visual critical mass. With works hung salon-style to cover every inch of the gallery—the once-cobwebbed corners to the hinges of the back door—the result was, indeed, overwhelming: A visual flurry of chaos matched only by its instant adoration by the region's public. It was, in fact, almost *too* successful, with around 900 people waiting in line up to 30 minutes to attend its September 2008 opening night.

But the more subtle aspect of the show comes from its catalog of the artists and their work, funded by a Regional Grant. By necessity it, too, is huge. But rather than mere keepsake, the book serves as something of an actual *catalog* of Pittsburgh art—a reference guide to 250 of the region's working artists, complete with biographical and contact information, sent to 1,000 galleries and art spaces across the country. These mailings were targeted so that, for example, when the catalog was sent to a space similar to Pittsburgh's Mattress Factory—which specializes in installation art—regional artists like Tim Kaulen from the South Side Sculpture Project, were highlighted.

Larson knows the catalog won't overwhelm its audience the same way that the show did, but that the result will be the same: A greater acknowledgement of the Pittsburgh region's art scene, both outside the region and within it.

"We want it to be useful as a tool," says Larson. "So that a photography gallery can be introduced to Pittsburgh photographers, and then contact those artists directly. And it's a way to network—to demystify some of the concepts people might have about the arts in this region."

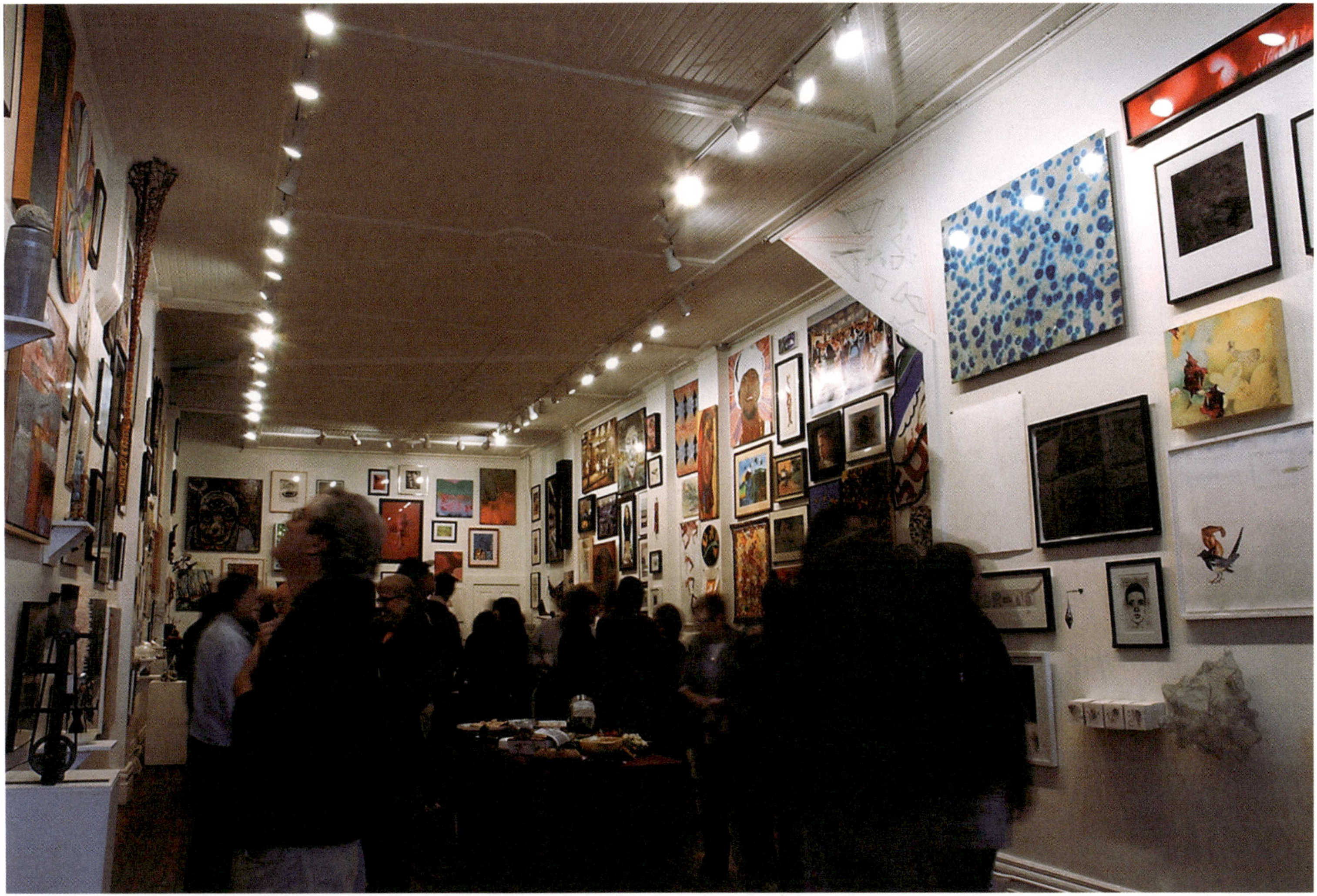

Doctor Jazz

Why are you so excited about the burgeoning new jam sessions in Pittsburgh?

A lot of young people ask me, 'Where did you discover jazz,' and I just say, 'huh?' It was in the *air* when I was born; it was the soundtrack of the community. My generation was very fortunate to come along at a time when jazz was appreciated, and I want to transmit that experience to the younger generation. In the clubs of the highlight era, you never knew who was going to walk through the door— I met Miles Davis just standing at the jukebox at the Crawford Grill! I want young people today to have something like that. And it's starting to get that feel—people are going out to get exposed to the creative act, *in vivo*, and meanwhile outside the clubs, on the sidewalk, there's a virtual university going on, with musicians and fans talking about music.

Those connections, and passing along the jazz history that goes with them, are one reason you've started the online networking site, the Pittsburgh Jazz Network?

I originally thought I was going one direction with Musicians of Wylie Avenue, with oral histories and archives. But with 'Web 2.0' platforms, I can manage all of those histories online. I could put that into a book or on a DVD, but on the web I can do all of that *and* I can take a picture or a movie in a club and send it right to the site. I have the fortune of being both historically aware, and an active participant. So I have thousands of photos and tapes—I've begun going through just photos of the old Hill District venue, the Crawford Grill, and just that is hours and hours of work. But on the Pittsburgh Jazz Network, people can post things from their archives, and they will all be annotated—the web can handle all of that.

So the jam sessions and the Jazz Network are really working to reopen lines of communication?

At some point, jazz music changed to a model that's not part of its tradition—it's closed now; promoters have kept the musicians and audiences separate, and that's anathema to the music. This isn't the symphony! In fact, one of the reasons jazz musicians get paid so little now is that nobody knows what we do. You never see a panel of musicians talking about jazz the way you see people dissect the 'Immaculate Reception' or the Steelers' last game. Sure, we talk about music every time we get together, but we haven't been sharing that knowledge with the public. Now, with the Network, it all opens up. If fans want to get to an artist, they don't have to go through layers of third parties—on the Network, you can go directly to anybody.

When he walks into one of Pittsburgh's jazz jam sessions, it's as though **Dr. Nelson Harrison** is going home. Watching the city's best and brightest musicians gather to play and talk, many of them Harrison's own former students, he imagines these young players commune with the ghosts of jazz history that still inhabit Pittsburgh. They're spirits he remembers: trombonist Harrison played his first gigs in 1954, and has continued playing and teaching for the ensuing half century, working with the likes of Nathan Davis and the Count Basie Big Band. But Harrison's enthusiasm has been subdued at times by a lack of recognition and respect for Pittsburgh's hallowed jazz ground—a shortcoming that has begun to be rectified with a series of projects aimed at reviving the spirit of Pittsburgh's jazz era by dignifying the past, educating the present, and connecting to the future of musicians in this city. With his Musicians of Wylie Avenue project, named for the famous Hill District street on which so much of Pittsburgh's jazz history was made, Harrison hopes to teach young musicians how to make their own golden age.

№ **58**\100   Jay Bee Model Circus   Awarded: $5,000

Trapeze Artist

When Jimmy Bashline died on May 15, 2008, at the age of 90, he left behind a legacy of visionary art that conjures the entirety of a specific cultural time and place—the highlight-era of the American circus, as seen in his hometown of Butler. Over the course of seven decades, Bashline's commercial work, as a cartoonist and sign painter, and non-commercial artwork stood as icons of Americana within his community. Only a month before his passing, Bashline's masterpiece—the Jay Bee Model Circus—opened at its permanent home at the Butler County Historical Society Heritage Center, its purchase and display by the Society funded by a Grassroots Grant.

The Jay Bee Model Circus is a diorama of over 1,000 hand-carved figurines, vehicles, animals, buildings, model trains and other mechanical implements, created entirely by self-taught artist Bashline. After spending World War II as an army airbrush artist, upon his return to Butler in 1946, he began what would become a lifelong process of hand-carving the figures for his Jay Bee Circus—everything from an elephant that splashes water to the individually carved spokes on the wagon wheels.

But the Jay Bee Model Circus isn't just about the fantasy world of the circus. It's about the real world of Butler at a time when the trains would periodically stop by filled with elephants and lions, and when the firm ground around P.J. Oesterling's feed shop would periodically give way to the firmament of the trapeze. That's why Bashline's fantastic circus environment isn't disrupted by the representation of real people—like Jimmy and his daughter Aryl, identifiable by the tiny glasses on her one-inch-tall figurine. Rather, it's strengthened, a chaos controlled by the town that's at its core.

"At our home, the circus was only seen by less than 200 visitors over the years," says Aryl Bashline. "The day of the grand opening, it was seen by over 700 people. So I think this is a wonderful venue for my father's extraordinary hobby. I hope it will continue to be enjoyed by citizens and other visitors to Butler County for years to come."

Bashline's artwork combined a long-term commitment with a detailed eye for the traits that comprised his concept of America. "Art," as Ralph Waldo Emerson said, "is the path of the creator to his work," a concept illustrated voluminously by Bashline, whose artwork thrived cathartically on detailed thematic repetition. His was an American oeuvre, a labor of love born from a Yankee love of labor and a passion for the subtle details hidden within the brash pomp and pride of Americana.

Jimmy Bashline worked on the Jay Bee Model Circus for 60 years, and lived long enough to see it find its permanent home. He knew what he loved to do, and he did it well for over half a century—and to that, we say "Bravo."

09: LORE

THE LIVES THESE PEOPLE LED AND THE STORIES THEY HAVE TO TELL ARE SO REMARKABLE.

Memory. Tradition. Collection.

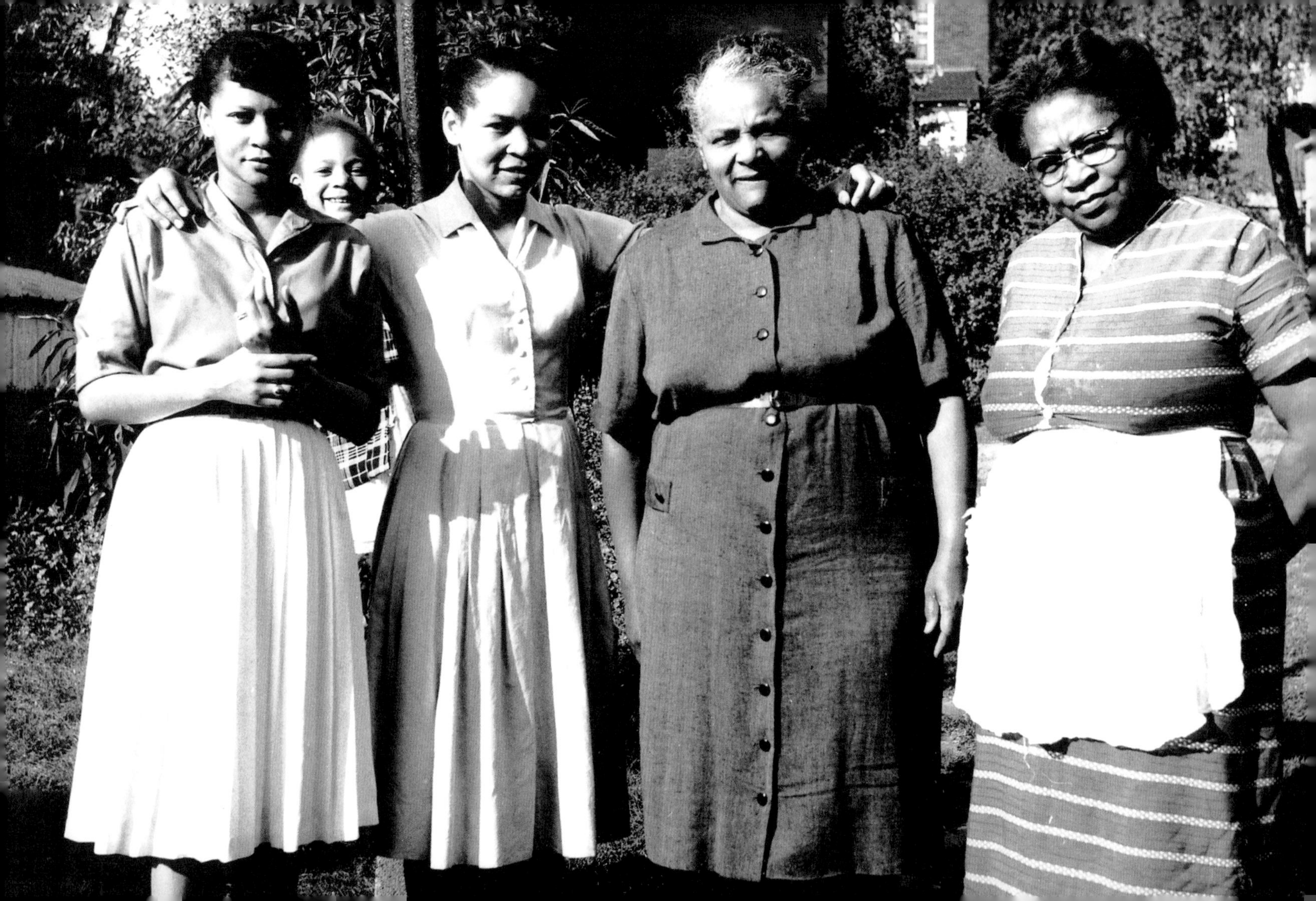

There is a folk song that tells us that, "along with the shoes and the shirts and the ties / there's a library that's lost when an old man dies." But as a part of Pittsburgh 250, several major Community Connections projects made it their mission to alleviate some small pieces of that loss—to preserve for future generations those "libraries" in our neighbors' minds that, together, form the place we call home.

The region's African-American history and artistic heritage; the largely unknown tale of Pittsburgh's role in the women's rights movement; the stories of the relationship between Southwestern Pennsylvanians and their environment: These are libraries of stories held as precious by our region's people. Through recorded interviews, Community Connections oral history projects shared those accounts, and used them as a foundation from which the region will continue to build its narrative in the future.

A SOLID FOUNDATION

The first-floor of the August Wilson Center for African American Culture in Pittsburgh was built on a foundation of stories: The tales of men and women, ordinary and extraordinary, from the Pittsburgh region. But by collecting the words and images of Pittsburgh's African-American artists and ordinary citizens alike through the Civil Rites oral history project, the Center hasn't just built an entrance-level exhibit. It's built a relationship with the community that will pay dividends for years.

To Shay Wafer, those stories and histories of the African-American experience in Pittsburgh were more than just tales; they're her reason for being here. Wafer moved to Pittsburgh to become the August Wilson Center's vice president of programs because of her love for Wilson's plays. But today's Pittsburgh, she soon discovered, is just as full of those kinds of vibrant life stories. With the Civil Rites project and its resultant exhibits, she and her colleagues have the opportunity to tell their neighbors that, just like Wilson's examination of the Hill District, their stories are important, too.

Throughout 2008, the August Wilson Center held a series of oral history "collecting fairs" in communities including McKees Rocks, Brookline, and Pittsburgh's North Side, inviting people to bring their stories, photos, and documents. While some participants sat in a private room, giving taped interviews, others had their photographs scanned on the spot—and left with both their originals, and their own digital version on CD. By the end of the series, its closing fairs in the Hill District and East Liberty were attracting large numbers of participants. But at the project's start, things weren't so easy—the Center encountered one of the most common roadblocks in oral history collection.

"We certainly encountered the attitude—'my story's not important, you don't want me,'" says Wafer. "But who deems whose stories are important? And why? We learned quickly that we had to go door-to-door in the neighborhoods, hand someone a flier face-to-face, and then explain the project. We tried to teach people what it means to collect—that their history *is* important. And by doing that, we created a groundswell of interest in contributing stories."

Collecting oral histories of Pittsburgh's African-American community is by no means a new idea: At Carnegie Mellon University, the Center for African-American Urban Studies and the Economy—under the leadership of History Department Chair Dr. Joseph Trotter—has made the city a national model for such collection. With the help of Trotter's system of questioning, a broad-based approach that offers an interviewer the means to peel back the layers of a person's story, the August Wilson Center was able to surmount some of the roadblocks facing those who would research these communities.

But the other big problem facing any oral historian is one that can't be solved by any means other than hard work: Time is not on their side. The generations, for example, that experienced the civil rights movement are slipping away. For that reason, in addition to their collecting fairs, Civil Rites sought out specific people within the community, concentrating on artists born in the region during the 1920s and '30s, such as internationally acclaimed sculptor Thaddeus Mosley, a New Castle native and Pittsburgh resident.

"Our list was prioritized by age, by people we *had* to get to," says Wafer. "Who's still out there? Who is an elder in the community? Who do we really need to get to—and get to quickly."

Through Civil Rites, the August Wilson Center established an oral history collection of the African-American experience in Southwestern Pennsylvania that serves not just as an archive, but as a proactive tool. The permanent exhibit, relying heavily on audio and visual components, tells the story of black life in the Steel City including recordings of oral histories collected by the project. By switching the recordings regularly, and contacting the interviewees to let them know when their story is being featured, the Center inspires the idea that it isn't just for the people, it's of the people.

"We wanted the community to have a sense of ownership—about this exhibit, and about this building," says Wafer. "As a new organization, in a new building, that was critical for us, and what better way to achieve it than to tell people, 'your stories, your pictures, they're in the exhibit—you *are* the exhibit.'"

HER STORY

Picture a map of America with lines drawn connecting the country's three largest cities: New York City to Chicago to Los Angeles. So many of the nation's historic movements can find their roots and branches in these three hubs, and the women's movement in the 1960s and '70s is no different.

But Dr. Patricia Ulbrich wants people to see that map slightly differently—with a detour through Western Pennsylvania, without which the women's movement would've been a very different historical event.

"Everybody knows New York was a hub," says Ulbrich. "Everyone knows Chicago, and L.A. Say that 'Pittsburgh was the fourth hub,' though, and people don't realize that. But there were extraordinary things that happened here, and extraordinary people."

Eleanor Smeal, Activist

Nº: 05\100   In Sisterhood: The Women's Movement in Pittsburgh   Awarded: $45,000

With In Sisterhood: The Women's Movement in Pittsburgh, Ulbrich took a step towards capturing the stories of those extraordinary people, and changing that traditional map of American women's rights history. Working with the Thomas Merton Center, and with the help of a Regional Grant, Ulbrich and a team of interviewers, photographers, and videographers collected a series of in-depth oral histories from some of the most important players in the '60s-to-'80s era of the Pittsburgh women's movement and created a touring multimedia exhibit.

"When you read histories of the women's movement, Pittsburgh is never mentioned," said Ulbrich. "It's important to tell the story so that it becomes a part of the national history. And it was important to do it for Pittsburgh 250, so that the anniversary included the legacy of women who acted as change agents."

Those change agents include people such as Eleanor Smeal, one of three women from Pittsburgh to serve as the national president of the National Organization for Women. It includes Gerald Gardner and JoAnn Evansgardner, whose complaint against the Pittsburgh *Press* for its discriminatory sex-segregated jobs listings went all the way to the Supreme Court and set the national legal precedent.

"The next day, newspapers all across the country were required to abandon segregating employment ads on the basis of sex," said Ulbrich.

In Sisterhood's histories go on to discuss the founding of Pittsburgh Action Against Rape, only the second rape-victim's advocacy organization in the country, and the University of Pittsburgh's Women's Studies program—another second in the nation—both founded in 1972.

"In 1977, feminist press KNOW, Inc., documented that there were 48 feminist organizations in Southwestern Pennsylvania," says Ulbrich. "With In Sisterhood, we looked at the ones that were really cutting edge—and what prompted those people to start them."

Like it was for the staff at the August Wilson Center, the necessity of moving swiftly in collecting oral histories became starkly apparent during In Sisterhood's work. The project was well into the process of conducting interviews when Ulbrich learned of the death of Jean Witter, the author of a historic 1979 legal opinion regarding the proposed Equal Rights Amendment and a woman whom In Sisterhood was scheduled to interview.

Witter's passing, however, only redoubled Ulbrich's efforts to fully capture the stories, the lives, and the energy of its subjects. Rather than a broad collection of short interviews, In Sisterhood's work examined a small number of key individuals, each of whom was studied with the concentration that their past efforts deserved.

"We spent at least five or six hours of interview time with each person," says Ulbrich. "It's a survey of the person's entire life—a set of themes about family origins, how that shaped them; how they became involved in the women's movement; what activities they engaged in. I want audiences to be inspired that people from right here in Pittsburgh—people from working-class backgrounds—were these kinds of change agents."

Once its touring options are exhausted, it will join other oral histories in the archive at the University of Pittsburgh.

"It is a phenomenal resource," says Ulbrich, "because the lives these people led and the stories they have to tell are so remarkable."

FIELD RECORDINGS

The history of Southwestern Pennsylvanians' relationship to the environment is one told in obvious contradictions and unlikely comrades. It's one of black smoke thickly clouding the skies, and of beautiful land stretching as far as the eye can see. It is of Cambria County's "coal is king" era, and Rachel Carson finding fossils in the grass of her backyard, across the river from Blakeian "dark, Satanic mills."

So it can't be too surprising that when Allegheny Front, a Pittsburgh-based radio show focusing on environmental issues, went to interview employees at the Pennsylvania Department of Environmental Protection (DEP), they discovered people like Donna Davis—a DEP Sewage Planning Specialist Supervisor.

"I wouldn't trade this job for anything in the world, even for more money," says Davis in an interview recorded and broadcast by Allegheny Front. "It's really the career I've dreamed of.

"I'd been working there maybe two or three years and one day we were slogging through mud up to our thighs to get to this break to sample it," Davis' interview continues. Her co-worker turned and said, "'I didn't know this job was going to be so glamorous!' It's not a job that a lot of people would do."

In her long employment at the DEP, Davis has overseen vast changes in Southwestern Pennsylvania's environment, from the industrial issues of the 1980s to today's more environ-mentally friendly culture. And within those stories are histories of a different sort, like Davis' anecdotes about being a woman inspecting the male-dominated world of the steel mills.

Glamorous, it may not be, but Davis' interview is just the kind of story that Allegheny Front Executive Producer Kathy Knauer hoped for when the group launched the Environmental Oral History Project, supported by a Regional Grant. Throughout 2008, Allegheny Front visited counties in the region, collecting interviews with people about their relationship with the environment.

For six months, the program's employees, interns and volunteers visited outdoor-related locations and events to record more than 125 stories of everyday Pennsylvanians. The result was a breadth of people, places, and stories from

Schenley Park, Pittsburgh

environmental professionals to ordinary citizens' recollections of their relationship to the outdoors. People like Glenn Helbling, a Squirrel Hill resident who constantly finds new things to enjoy in Pittsburgh's Schenley Park, or 10-year-old Brendan Glover of Rural Valley, Armstrong County, who loves to go fishing and "listen to the sounds, see nature, see how fish and birds act when they're just being left alone."

Sometimes, however, those memories are of surmounting the odds stacked by a legacy of industrialization. Diane Lindley of Lone Pine, Washington County, recounts the struggle her mother and father went through when their home was nearly destroyed by the collapse of an old longwall coal mine. "I believe that politicians won't act until the people take a stand," Lindley told Allegheny Front. "We have streams on our property that feed into a bigger stream, and then into a bigger river, and eventually, the water you see at the Point in Pittsburgh comes from all these little streams. Well, when the undermining destroys that, it's a problem for everyone."

Many of these interviews were edited and broadcast on Allegheny Front's weekly radio program, produced at community-supported radio station WYEP-FM in Pittsburgh, and the vast majority of the interviews were made available for online listening on the program's website.

The project took to heart Community Connections' mission of building new relationships between disparate elements of the region by using other funded projects to uncover interview possibilities. Amongst their many outings, Allegheny Front used events held by Fisherman's Tale, Wild Waterways Conservancy, Venture Outdoors, and the Mobile Agricultural Education Lab—all projects supported by Community Connections—to find unique perspectives on interactions between people and their environment.

The message of these environmental oral histories is a simple one: Our everyday lives aren't just worthy of history, they're vital to history. And they're stories that must be told, heard, and kept.

"Over the course of the Environmental Oral History Project, it became evident that these are ordinary people, and their normal lives involve the environment and nature every day," says Knauer. "I think the message is that what we have here in Southwestern Pennsylvania is pretty wonderful and it belongs to everyone."

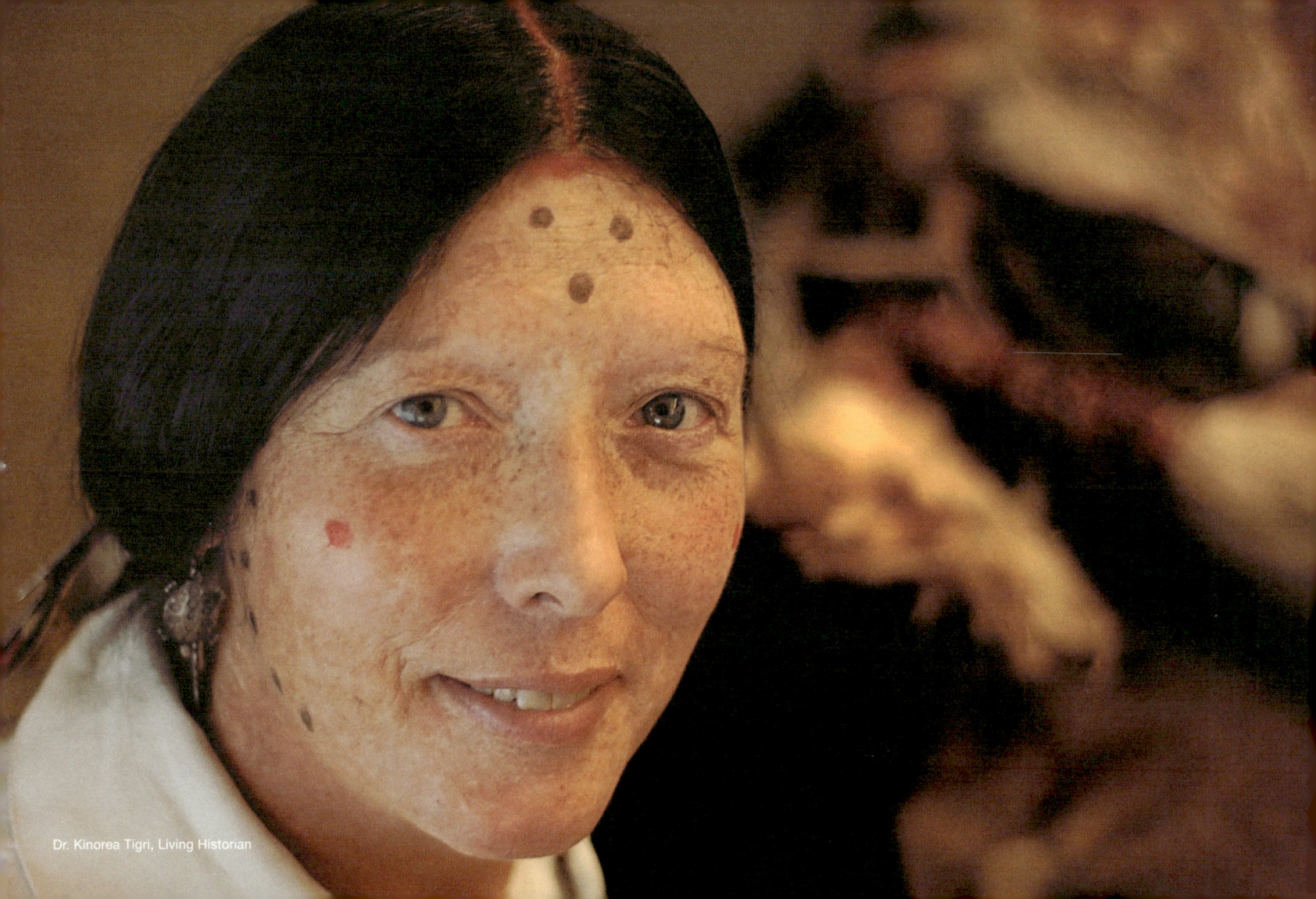

Dr. Kinorea Tigri, Living Historian

History Booking

When Westmoreland Heritage Executive Director Tom Headley speaks of the 18th century, you'd be forgiven for thinking it's only just happened. Fort Ligonier, the Battle of Bushy Run, French soldiers, Indian warriors and shamans—Headley refers to them all in the present tense. And that's not just historian's prerogative: Tom Headley doesn't just know *about* French and Indian War soldiers, he *knows* them.

For the Westmoreland County History Speakers Program, begun with funding from a Grassroots Grant, Headley is in constant contact with a variety of living historians—portraying Native Americans, 18th-century soldiers, and an array of other characters from the region's past whom he connects with schools and classes, history clubs and small cultural organizations.

Westmoreland County is an area steeped in history—and of particular historical importance to the founding of Pittsburgh, being a vital stop on the Forbes Trail. But the issues it faces, even within projects directly addressing that history, are as modern as anywhere else. Because, as Headley points out, while Westmoreland County is chock-full of historical sites and amenities, the days when a school group's field trip was a given are long gone.

"Schools don't have a big budget for supplemental things these days," says Headley. "Because of money or because it's not a curriculum priority, some schools no longer do field trips to these sites. We empower the sites to approach these schools, and tell them, 'we can send a living historian *into* the school.'"

Through the speakers program, Westmoreland Heritage and the Westmoreland County Historical Society have connected school programs with living historians, and other speakers to more than 25 of the county's historical and cultural societies. Headley sees this as part of Heritage's mission to better market history as a regional amenity. The speakers' project brings groups, patrons, and historians together towards that goal. "There's an economic benefit to marketing history in a more unified way," says Headley, "and alongside education, that's another part of our mission."

The speakers, however, have a much more straightforward mission when they visit a school or an organization: By acting as an example of actual early-Western Pennsylvania life, they offer a glimpse of the past that's less a page out of a history book, and more a page out of history.

"When someone like Dr. Kinorea Tigri—a Native American living historian—goes into a school, it's a different way to get to kids thinking and learning about history; a way that grabs their attention."

10: MOMENTUM

THE BEAUTY OF THIS IS THAT IT TURNED OUT TO BE THE TIP OF THE ICEBERG.

Build. Establish. Grow.

Community clean-up volunteers, Allegheny County

No schoolyard bell rang on January 1, 2009, marking the end of Pittsburgh 250.

There was no finish-line tape for the region to collectively crash through as the 250th year passed into the 251st. Most importantly, the people, projects, and motivations that together comprised Community Connections didn't sit back in relief once this momentous year in Pittsburgh's history technically ended. Instead, the work carries on because the pressing needs of a region don't watch the calendar.

For some of the 100 projects involved in Community Connections, their work was specifically tied in to Pittsburgh 250. But even though events such as Won't You Be My Neighbor? Days and the French and Indian War reenactments at Boyce Park and Fort McIntosh have ended, the roots that those organizations have planted in their communities will continue to grow from year to year.

For others, the work done in 2008 provided organizations with new, and often unexpected, opportunities. The new 18th-century style fortifications built at Old Bedford Village, for example, began by drawing living historians to the Village, but, by the end of 2008, it had Hollywood film producers scouting the location for period movies.

When Venture Outdoors began its Diversity Outdoors initiative as a Grassroots Project, with the goal of exposing more minority populations to the region's outdoor activities, the project was meant to be a one-year addendum to pre-existing community festivals.

"The beauty of this is that it turned out to be the tip of the iceberg," Sean Brady, assistant executive director of Venture Outdoors, says of Diversity Outdoors. "It got us thinking and planning how to reach new communities for outdoor recreation and environmental education."

Diversity Outdoors saw the organization take climbing walls, trailers full of bikes, fishing-related activities and more to festivals in Pittsburgh neighborhoods such as East Liberty, the North Side, and the Hill District to reach populations often cut off from outdoor activities by geography and transportation options—or, as Venture Outdoors discovered, simply by long-held cultural perceptions.

"It's not just an economic barrier that keeps diverse populations from enjoying outdoor recreation," says Brady. "It's cultural barriers—the belief, from what people see, that these activities are only a Caucasian experience. It makes some feel like they need special permission just to go into the park or use the city's trails."

But Venture Outdoors also discovered two other facts: This issue isn't a local one, but a national problem, and yet there were no established approaches to address it. With its new organization-wide Inclusivity Initiative, Venture Outdoors seeks to reflect the diversity of the community it serves. Building upon their Grassroots Grant, the group sought extensive funding from foundations and corporations for a three-year initiative to find successful ways to raise minority participation, beginning with the award of a $30,000 grant from a major outdoors-wear company.

Just as Diversity Outdoors marked only the beginning of a successful new initiative, the Grove City College Philanthropy Project began during Pittsburgh 250, but its work is set to grow for years to come. The project's idea was simple: Give a classroom of college students money, and let them invest it in the community as they see fit.

Trusted with resources, students were also given a hands-on lesson in how the nonprofit sector operates and were exposed to the many ways that local challenges are being met by worthy organizations.

Communications Professor Jennifer Scott had $4,000 for her class to disperse, acquired through a Grassroots Grant. But before that first class had finished researching nonprofit organizations in the Grove City Area or made funding decisions, Grove City College had already acquired funding to keep the Philanthropy Project going for another year.

"Without the funding from Community Connections, we wouldn't have been able to launch the project," says project manager and Grove City College Development Officer, Brian Powell. "Then we leveraged that into further funding for two more classes in the Spring semester, and at least three more classes next year!"

But Scott and Powell's aspirations go farther than 2009: The plan is to use these classes as a baseline, with assessments and data from those courses making the case to add philanthropic giving as a regular core program that Grove City offers its students in perpetuity.

"The project offers other avenues to allow students who've graduated from these philanthropy classes to take it to the next level," says Powell. "The question is 'How do we develop this into a whole initiative, for the campus, and for the region?'"

The Philanthropy Project is one of a handful of like projects being funded and watched through Campus Compact, a national service-learning organization, which wishes to bring philanthropic education to a national level. And, regionally, a similar course has begun at the University of Pittsburgh's Graduate School of Public and International Affairs, which both Powell and Scott have helped with idea exchanges.

For many projects, the regional scope and far-reaching prestige of Pittsburgh 250 and Community Connections opened doors that had previously been tightly shut, and allowed new ideas and new relationships to prosper—along with the projects themselves.

At Slippery Rock University (SRU), the plan was to use a Grassroots Grant to help purchase new bicycles for the Green Bikes Initiative, as part of Slippery Rock Green and Growing— a project that couples the lending of free bikes together with a campus-wide tree-planting movement. But the grant from Community Connections provided much more than needed financial support. Attention from outside their immediate community and participation in Pittsburgh 250 helped the group to leverage further grants and carry the project beyond their initial plans.

"We were able to get a lot of unrelated groups involved, from the University's president on down," says Diana Wolak, SRU's cooperative activities assistant. "The president was so impressed by the prestige that came from this grant, he really

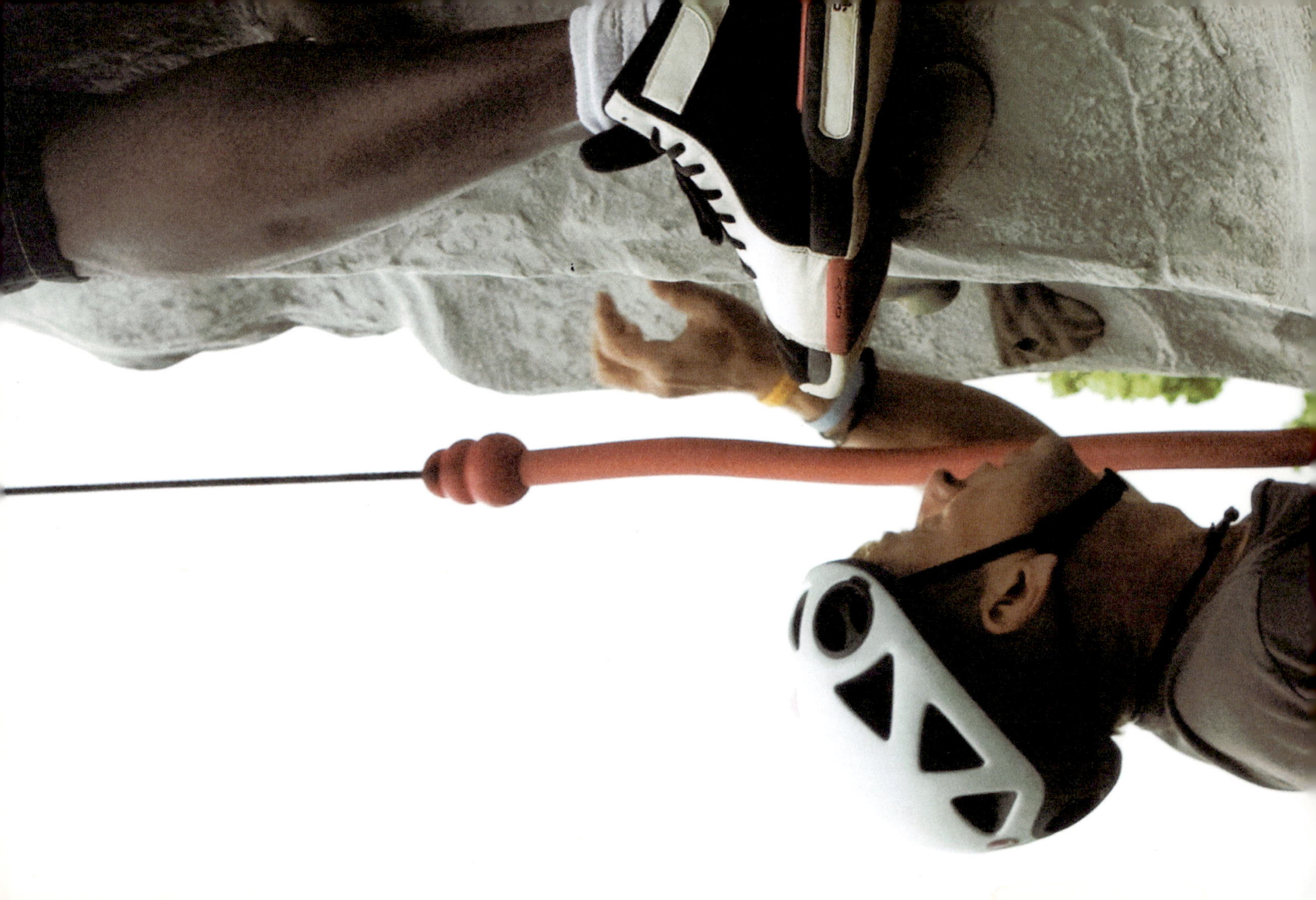

No 18\100 Diversity Outdoors Awarded: $5,000

bought into the idea and provided matching funds — then we got another matching grant from a local company."

By the time the project officially launched at the end of September, Green and Growing had already surpassed its dream goal of 10 new bikes — there are 14 new and plenty of refurbished old green bikes on campus today — and had planted 100 trees on SRU's campus. Cycling Club advisor, and SRU's coordinator of outdoor adventures, Steve Roberts was even able to commit paid student hours to bike repair and other project-related work. And with the continued publicity garnered through its Pittsburgh 250 connections, Green and Growing will keep on doing just that well beyond 2008's official celebration of the anniversary.

"We had 12 articles published about this project since receiving our grant," says Wolak. "Which is a *lot* in Slippery Rock. And a lot of the attention we've received is because we received a grant from Pittsburgh. And now, the fact that there's money being spent on the project that *isn't* coming from the grant, that speaks to how people think this will sustain over time."

For Lizette Olsen, executive director of Mercer County AWARE, the area's domestic and sexual violence advocacy center, a Grassroots Grant meant a bold new approach to subsequent funders.

"Being up in Mercer County, we didn't anticipate actually getting the grant in the first place," says Olsen. "We felt really surprised and validated when we received that grant — and, in particular, it helped so much in leveraging other support."

By midway through 2008, that had translated into a $10,000 grant from the United Way to continue and expand upon the work started with AWARE's program educating students and teachers in Grove City schools. AWARE estimates that it now reaches 45 percent of all students, including 71 percent of all high school students. It's no comparison to the previous year, when AWARE's programming was all but absent from the school district.

№: **60**\100   **Slippery Rock University Green and Growing**   Awarded: $5,000

Moreover, the organization has a whole new sphere of regional relationships to build upon. It's not just that Olsen can now talk to new corporations and foundations about support; her staff can honestly tell children in danger that there are people out there—not just in Mercer County, but all over—who care about their future.

Olsen knew the importance of such cross-border investment for herself, but had it reinforced by a conversation with one of the students that AWARE staff member Jaimie Kratochvil visited throughout the year. She explained to the student that people were coming from Pittsburgh to visit the organization—and that money from Pittsburgh allowed the meetings with Jaimie to happen.

"The concept that strangers down there in Pittsburgh would pay for a staff member to visit this student—it blew her away," says Olsen. "This student will be able to see Jaimie through the balance of the school year and beyond. I explained how the relationship was supported—and important—to people from outside the county, and this student was so surprised that she asked me, 'Wow—I matter?'

"How do you measure the impact of a student who did not have relief or support, who now can begin to trust adults again? How do you measure a more positive vision of the future?"

Lizette Olsen, Youth Advocate

Moments like these—when we realize with startling immediacy just how closely linked our lives have become with those around us—are moments that alter our understanding of what it means to be a responsible community member, a caring neighbor, and an engaged fellow citizen.

While it may have begun as an initiative to enliven the celebration of a city's founding anniversary, Community Connections became much more than that. By bringing new people to the table and amplifying their voices during a year of reflection and aspiration, the initiative not only gave people a stake in commemorating the region's past, but also planted seeds for the future.

"The vibrancy and feeling of possibility that's in the Pittsburgh region—it's almost palpable," says co-chair Aradhna Dhanda.

Neither a beginning nor an ending, Community Connections instead has been another gateway through which Southwestern Pennsylvania has traveled to emerge only more resolute. And, what's more, the initiative built a regional network of connections that will last far beyond Pittsburgh 250.

"The process behind Community Connections was just as valuable as the projects it supported," says co-chair Cathy Lewis Long. "For the first time, at the grassroots level, we have begun knitting together the communities of Southwestern Pennsylvania."

Ultimately, what Community Connections produced is something more than the sum of its 100 funded projects, more than the number of people who applied or dollars that were awarded. Rather, the program laid the groundwork for continued collaboration, mutual support, and greater awareness among all of the region's constituent parts.

"I can't tell you where it's going," says co-chair George Miles. "But I hope that when somebody looks back someday, they'll be able to say, 'That was the start—that's when people started being proud to be a part of this region. Not just their part of it, but as a whole.'"

New social and economic ventures that lead to new relationships between neighbors and communities, a greater understanding of the connections between the grassroots and the treetops, a Southwestern Pennsylvania whose counties are strengthened as much by their unique diversity as by their common interdependence: Community Connections helped to make Pittsburgh 250 about all of these things. Indeed, its most lasting outcome and immeasurable success will be these community connections, forged from the raw materials and natural resources that have always enabled this region to grow: the talent, energy, and imagination of its people.

APPENDIX

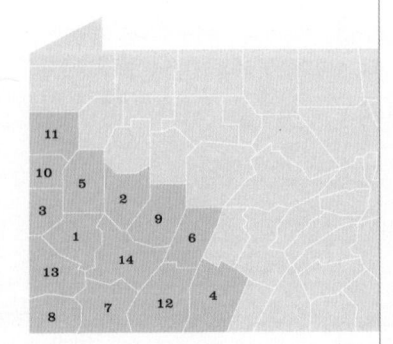

ALLEGHENY (1)
POPULATION: 1,219,210
AREA: 730 square miles
LARGEST CITY: Pittsburgh

The de facto center of the region and home to more than 40% of its people, Allegheny County is often thought of as synonymous with the City of Pittsburgh. But the county comprises a diverse wealth of historical and cultural contrasts—just consider the pastoral childhood home of environmental pioneer Rachel Carson in Springdale only a short distance away from the industrial acreage of the Allegheny River. Even Pittsburgh itself, consisting of 90 unique—and often fiercely independent—neighborhoods, is far more than just the sum of its intricate parts. This broad range of towns, neighborhoods, and communities is well illustrated by Allegheny's Community Connections projects.

ARMSTRONG (2)
POPULATION: 69,059
AREA: 654 square miles
LARGEST CITY: Kittanning

Home of roaring river runs and miles of hiking trails, a rich industrial history, as well as Parker, the "Smallest City in America," Armstrong County is something of a well-kept secret. Carved out of several adjacent counties in 1800, Armstrong remains somewhat obscured by its more populous neighbors. But the county cherishes its small towns and beautiful landscapes, as attested to by projects celebrating the outdoors and a long history of strong community bonds.

BEAVER (3)
POPULATION: 173,074
AREA: 435 square miles
LARGEST CITY: Aliquippa

Traced by rivers, dotted with parks and steeped in industrial history, Beaver County is something of a microcosm of Southwestern Pennsylvania. Located in the Northwest of the region, along the Ohio and West Virginia borders, Beaver hasn't struggled with the identity crisis of other border counties—proximity to Pittsburgh has seen to that. But such proximity has also seen Beaver County rise and fall with its southern neighbor, and has sought to balance its past with a new, greener future through its Community Connections revitalization projects.

BEDFORD (4)
POPULATION: 49,650
AREA: 1,015 square miles
LARGEST CITY: Bedford

Founded as one of the last major outposts on the Forbes Trail during the march on Fort Duquesne, Bedford is seen as Pittsburgh's lesser known, yet slightly older, brother city. So while Bedford County isn't always included in the Pittsburgh region, it was an obvious necessity for any celebration of Pittsburgh 250. Bedford County, located at the far Southeastern edge of the region, is the gateway for all roads leading into the region—be it the Turnpike or the Lincoln Highway—and its Community Connections projects reflected this significant history.

GREENE (8)
POPULATION: 39,503
AREA: 576 square miles
LARGEST CITY: Waynesburg

Tucked away in the Southwestern corner of the region, Greene County remains just as pristine as in its earliest days with majestic rolling hills and lush green valleys. At its heart, the city of Waynesburg truly could pass for a new "Eden" as its founder, Thomas Slater, named it when he first settled there in the late 18th century. The county's contributions to Community Connections reflect this pride in its built and natural surroundings, as well as the creativity and ingenuity of its people and the bright new minds coming out of Waynesburg University.

INDIANA (9)
POPULATION: 87,690
AREA: 830 square miles
LARGEST CITY: Indiana

Located in the Eastern-central part of the region, Indiana County is best known regionally for Indiana University of Pennsylvania, and nationally as the Christmas Tree Capital of America and the birthplace of actor Jimmy Stewart. A largely rural and sparsely populated area, Indiana County is known for its wealth of outdoor amenities and rich local history, two factors that Community Connections projects chose to highlight in 2008.

LAWRENCE (10)
POPULATION: 90,991
AREA: 360 square miles
LARGEST CITY: New Castle

Despite close social and historic ties to Youngstown in Eastern Ohio, Lawrence County and its principal city of New Castle have managed to carve out its own identity while still maintaining links to its neighbors to the West and South in Pittsburgh. Home to the Zambellis, the First Family of Fireworks, Lawrence County has strong community traditions dating back to the immigration of whole European villages in the 19th century. Lawrence County chose to commemorate 2008 by dedicating its Community Connections dollars to serving area children.

MERCER (11)
POPULATION: 116,809
AREA: 672 square miles
LARGEST CITY: Sharon

Mercer County, in the northernmost portion of the region, is often left out of the Southwestern Pennsylvania equation due to its proximity to Youngstown, Ohio, and to the Erie region. But historically, it's Mercer's ties to Pittsburgh—whether that's shoppers headed to its outlet stores or students at Grove City College—that keep this county connected to the region. While other population centers like Sharon and Greenville retain an urban character, Mercer is a largely rural county and many Community Connections projects sought to overcome the distances, both geographic and economic, that separate the people of the county.

*POPULATION STATISTICS FROM U.S. CENSUS BUREAU ESTIMATES FOR 2007.

BUTLER (5)

POPULATION: 181,934
AREA: 789 square miles
LARGEST CITY: Butler

Just 12 years after Allegheny County was incorporated, a northern portion of the County was carved off as Butler County and the two have been closely linked ever since. Whether it's the early discovery of oil in Petrolia Valley, the founding of AK Steel or the invention of the Bantam Jeep, Butler has cemented itself as a pillar of the region's industrial heritage. Its Community Connections projects balance the preservation of this storied past with an eagerness for the county to reinvent itself.

CAMBRIA (6)

POPULATION: 144,995
AREA: 688 square miles
LARGEST CITY: Johnstown

From the 19th-century flood that made Johnstown infamous, to the boom-times of heavy industry and king coal, to the more recent emergence of the defense industry and burgeoning arts communities, Cambria County has a character that is at once quintessentially Southwestern Pennsylvania, but at the same time uniquely independent. Whether restoring the robber baron grandeur of the historic homes in Ebensburg, or revitalizing post-industrial Johnstown, Cambria used Community Connections as an opportunity to seed its own rebirth.

FAYETTE (7)

POPULATION: 144,556
AREA: 790 square miles
LARGEST CITY: Uniontown

With a heritage stretching from the days of pioneers, Fayette County lives up to its namesake, Revolutionary War hero the Marquis de la Fayette. Founded in 1783, the county has since witnessed a steady stream of risk-taking settlers, beginning with the mountain men and women who first cleared the Laurel Highlands, to the heydays of the glass industry that helped build Connellsville, all the way through to the present with the ongoing revitalization of Uniontown. And as an integral part of the Great Allegheny Passage, Fayette County used Community Connections as an opportunity to display its mixture of classic Americana and scenic natural areas like Ohiopyle State Park to new visitors.

SOMERSET (12)

POPULATION: 77,861
AREA: 1,075 square miles
LARGEST CITY: Somerset

In the heart of the Laurel Highlands, Somerset County is home to the Flight 93 National Memorial, boasts two state parks, several state forests, and major skiing destinations. Combine these wilderness attractions with classic small-town charm in Somerset and Windber, and you've got one of the most attractive destinations for those looking to poke around the corners of the region and rediscover some hidden gems like the Arcadia Theater. An active county, some of its Community Connections projects focused on outdoor recreation and building community health.

WASHINGTON (13)

POPULATION: 205,553
AREA: 857 square miles
LARGEST CITY: Washington

As its name suggests, Washington County and its like-named principal city were named after the colonial colonel turned revolutionary general turned American President George Washington. Ironically, in 1794 Washington would send Federal troops into his namesake County to put down the infamous Whiskey Rebellion headquartered there. This rebellious spirit may be more tame today, but it still inspires many in Washington to challenge the county's most pressing issues.

WESTMORELAND (14)

POPULATION: 362,326
AREA: 1,023 square miles
LARGEST CITY: Greensburg

Central to the region, Westmoreland County is steeped in all the things that make up Southwestern Pennsylvania's unique character. Colonial battles and early American history? Check. Pioneering settlers and breadbasket agriculture? Check. Heavy industry and technological achievement? Check. No, Westmoreland County doesn't miss a thing. With classic American cities like Greensburg, Latrobe and Ligonier, Trail Towns of the Great Allegheny Passage, and leading social and environmental movements, Westmoreland's rich character was well-represented by equally diverse Community Connections projects.

Pittsburgh 250 Community Connections was a funding stream supporting 100 small-scale community-based projects in 14 counties of Southwestern Pennsylvania with programming throughout the year 2008 to commemorate the 250th anniversary of the founding of the Pittsburgh region.

Pittsburgh 250 Community Connections Regional Projects were 12 compelling initiatives that affected large audiences, left a lasting impact on communities, and contributed to the "Pride & Progress" of Southwestern Pennsylvania—the theme of Community Connections. Most projects received awards of $50,000 for their activities in 2008. Decisions were made by a panel of regional leaders that included representatives from all 14 counties.

Where additional details appear within the text of this book, page reference numbers are listed *(in italic)* after their description.

№: 01\100 Celebrate Pittsburgh: Music Commissioning Project Awarded: $50,000
River City Brass Band commissioned seven new Pittsburgh-themed musical works from seven regional composers. The new works premiered throughout 2008 and were featured during the River City Brass Band's performances at concert venues in eight communities in Allegheny, Beaver, Cambria, and Westmoreland counties. Project Manager: James Siders *(121–123)*

№: 02\100 Civil Rites: Oral Histories of Two Generations of Pittsburgh Artists Awarded: $50,000
August Wilson Center for African American Culture collected the work and personal stories of local African-American artists as well as the memories of those who knew them in a multimedia presentation that premiered at the Center's dedication in 2009 and became part of its permanent collection. Project Managers: Shay Wafer, Ada Griffin, and Neil Barclay *(134–135)*

№: 03\100 Explore Western Pennsylvania's Wild Waterways Awarded: $50,000
Wild Waterways Conservancy constructed a series of boat launches throughout Butler, Beaver, and Lawrence counties to create a more welcoming environment for residents and visitors to enjoy the waterways of the Connoquenessing and Slippery Rock watersheds. Project Managers: Frank Moone and Sheree Dougharty *(98)*

№: 04\100 Great Allegheny Passage Trail Town Public Art Project Awarded: $50,000
Progress Fund coordinated a community process to bring public art installations to each of six Trail Towns along the Great Allegheny Passage: Meyersdale, Rockwood, Confluence, Ohiopyle, Connellsville and West Newton. The project contributed to the ongoing community and economic development efforts in Fayette, Somerset, and Westmoreland counties. Project Managers: Cathy McCollom and Amy Camp *(44–45)*

№: 05\100 In Sisterhood: The Women's Movement in Pittsburgh Awarded: $45,000
Thomas Merton Center produced a first-of-its-kind multimedia exhibit featuring 20 influential leaders and activists in the women's movement with roots in Pittsburgh during the latter part of the 20th century. Project Manager: Dr. Patricia Ulbrich *(135–139)*

№: 06\100 In the Making: 250 Years/250 Artists Awarded: $35,000
Fe gallery created a museum-quality, full-color catalogue documenting a first-of-its-kind visual exhibition of artwork by 250 artists from all 14 counties in Southwestern Pennsylvania. The catalogue provided a showcase of regional artists to curators, museum trustees, and collectors through its distribution regionally and nationally. Project Manager: Jill Larson *(123–124)*

№: **07**\100   **Mobile Ag/Ed Science Lab**
Awarded: $50,000

PA Friends of Agriculture Foundation constructed a mobile science and agriculture laboratory to travel to schools throughout Southwestern Pennsylvania. Building on a previously successful model, the mobile learning environment brought the science of the farm directly into schools. Project Manager: Val Huston *(20–21)*

№: **08**\100   **Pittsburgh Environmental Oral History Project**   Awarded: $35,000

Allegheny Front, Western Pennsylvania's only environmental radio program, produced a series of personal stories, interviews, and features to celebrate the Pittsburgh region's environmental history and progress from a region based on resource extraction to a burgeoning leader in green environmental practices. Project Manager: Kathy Knauer *(139–141)*

№: **09**\100   **Pittsburgh Signs Project: 250 Signs of Western Pennsylvania**   Awarded: $50,000

Pittsburgh Signs Project created a 200-page, full-color book documenting unique signage from the 14 counties of Southwestern Pennsylvania to celebrate the unique culture of the region. The project captured the visual treasures of the area and shared them with a global audience both online and in the form of a brilliantly colored book. Project Managers: Jennifer Baron, Greg Langel, Elizabeth Perry, and Mark Stroup *(119–120)*

№: **10**\100   **Roadside Giants of the Lincoln Highway**   Awarded: $49,340

Lincoln Highway Heritage Corridor worked with vocational and technical students in Bedford, Somerset, and Westmoreland counties to design and build four incredible roadside attractions—Roadside Giants—at locations along Pennsylvania's historic Lincoln Highway. Project Manager: Olga Herbert *(42–43)*

№: **11**\100   **South Side Sculpture Project**
Awarded: $50,000

Industrial Arts Co-op completed the final stage of the South Side Sculpture, a monumental piece of public art created from salvaged artifacts of the local steel industry on the former J&L and LTV riverfront mill sites. The enormous sculpture used steel I-beams to depict the towering figures of two laboring steelworkers and will be placed on permanent public display along the Monongahela River in Pittsburgh's South Side. Project Manager: Tim Kaulen *(38–39)*

№: **12**\100   **Won't You Be My Neighbor? Days**
Awarded: $50,000

Family Communications, Inc. promoted a series of events honoring Fred Rogers on the 80th anniversary of his birth in March 2008. Won't You Be My Neighbor? Days featured free or reduced admission to many cultural and educational venues and events across the region and additional programming on how to be a good neighbor. Project Manager: Margy Whitmer *(82–84)*

Pittsburgh 250 Community Connections Grassroots Projects were 88 community initiatives led by community members in each of the 14 counties in Southwestern Pennsylvania. These projects involved local residents and organizations, focused on local interests, and demonstrated civic engagement and innovation at the grassroots level. Most projects received awards of $5,000 for their activities in 2008. Decisions were made by panels of community leaders convened in each county.

Following is a list of these 88 projects sorted by county of origin. Where additional details appear within the text of this book, page reference numbers are listed (in italic) after descriptions.

ALLEGHENY

Projects: 24 \ Total Awarded: $120,000

№: 13\100   Allegheny Market House Co-op   Awarded: $5,000
Allegheny Market House Co-op led its first membership drive, a necessary initial step in the establishment of a cooperative grocery for Pittsburgh's North Side communities. Project Managers: Brad Spencer and Elena Firsova

№: 14\100   Be Well! Pittsburgh   Awarded: $5,000
Be Well! improved uninsured Pittsburghers' health through education about available health care resources. The project distributed booklets and fliers on targeted health topics, gave presentations at related events, and made its resources available online. Project Manager: Jude Vachon (113)

№: 15\100   Bridge to Broadway   Awarded: $5,000
This beautification project revitalized the intersection linking Broadway, Pitcairn's main street, to the Norfolk Southern Rail Yard. Features included a decorative fence, landscaping, restoration of the original cobblestone driveway, and the placement of 10 plaques erected throughout Pitcairn in places of historical significance. Project Manager: Tom Barnishin

№: 16\100   Citywide Salon   Awarded: $5,000
Academy of the South Side hosted a month-long public showcase of works by Pittsburgh artists displayed in bus shelters throughout the city. Project Manager: Dan Vogel (120–121)

№: 17\100   Colonnade of History   Awarded: $5,000
Natrona Comes Together Association created a public art sculpture consisting of 12 concrete columns designed by local artists and arranged in two rows to form the entrance to the new Natrona Park. Project Manager: Bill Godfrey

№: 18\100   Diversity Outdoors   Awarded: $5,000
Venture Outdoors connected minority communities in Pittsburgh with greater access to outdoor recreation opportunities. The project encouraged healthy lifestyles and promoted environmental awareness by improving access to outdoor amenities, bringing recreational equipment to neighborhood festivals, and organizing outdoor events and activities. Project Manager: Sean Brady (148)

№: 19\100   East of Liberty   Awarded: $5,000
Hyperboy Media produced community screenings of *East of Liberty*, a documentary series that gave voice to residents and business owners in Pittsburgh's East Liberty neighborhood in light of rapid changes brought on by ongoing redevelopment. Project Manager: Chris Ivey (91)

№: 20\100   Fisherman's Tale   Awarded: $5,000
Lemington Community Services organized fishing trips along Pittsburgh's rivers and in rural creeks surrounding the city for an underserved population of African American senior citizens. Participants were able to enjoy the outdoors and establish new social connections. Project Managers: Joy Starzl and Arnold Perry (96–98)

№: 22\100 **Grant Avenue Pocket Park**
Awarded: $5,000

New Sun Rising created a public green space in the heart of the Millvale downtown business district. Cleaning up a community eyesore, this green space provided a place to relax, meet with friends, and enjoy community and artistic events. Project Managers: Brian Wolovich and Eddie Figas *(72–75)*

№: 23\100 **Greetings from Pittsburgh: Neighborhood Narratives** Awarded: $5,000

This series of nine short narrative films portraying the experience, character, and stories of the diverse neighborhoods of Pittsburgh was created by filmmakers who live in and take pride in their neighborhoods. Project Managers: Andrew Halasz and Kristen Lauth Schaeffer *(86–89)*

№: 24\100 **Homewood Redd Up!** Awarded: $5,000

Operation Better Block, on behalf of the Homewood, Squirrel Hill, Point Breeze, and Park Place Redd Up Coalition, hosted several three-day cooperative community clean up weekends in the Homewood and Squirrel Hill neighborhoods of Pittsburgh. Project Managers: Aliyah Durham and Khalif Ali *(69–70)*

№: 25\100 **Keepin' it Real: Black Athletes and Racism in Pittsburgh Sports** Awarded: $5,000

Rights and Responsibilities documented the experiences of African American athletes in Pittsburgh: their achievements, their troubles, and their thoughts about issues of race and sports in the region. The locally-produced film was screened in communities along with panel discussions and audience participation. Project Manager: Aisha White

№: 26\100 **Lawrenceville Historic House Tour: Snapshots Through Time** Awarded: $5,000

Lawrenceville Stakeholders and the Lawrenceville Historic Society expanded the Lawrenceville Hospitality House Tour to spotlight historic residences in Pittsburgh's Lawrenceville neighborhood. Additionally, the project staged a series of reenactments and performances at historic locations such as the Allegheny Arsenal and the Allegheny Cemetery. Project Managers: Josh and Kate Bayer

№: 27\100 **MLK Community Mural Project**
Awarded: $5,000

KH Design Studio created a Pittsburgh 250-themed portion of the large MLK Community Mural Project, an expansive series of murals painted in communities along the Martin Luther King Busway throughout the East End neighborhoods of Pittsburgh. Project Manager: Kyle Holbrook

№: 28\100 **Musicians of Wylie Avenue**
Awarded: $5,000

Culling the history of jazz musicians and famous venues along the Hill District's celebrated Wylie Avenue, the project used documentary sources including archival materials, interviews with jazz musicians, and eyewitness accounts of this historic era to help establish the Pittsburgh Jazz Network online community. Project Manager: Dr. Nelson Harrison *(126–127)*

№: 29\100 **Out of this Furnace: New Tales of Labor and Unions** Awarded: $5,000

Unseam'd Shakespeare Company collected oral histories and hosted community workshops in Braddock in conjunction with its 2008 production of *Out of this Furnace*, a theatrical adaptation of Thomas Bell's classic tale of immigrant laborers during Pittsburgh's steel industry heyday. Project Manager: Tim Dawson *(85–86)*

№: 30\100 **Pittsburgh Safe Neighborhoods**
Awarded: $5,000

Pittsburgh Community Reinvestment Group continued research and convened community forums to help implement city-wide public safety initiatives such as a grassroots block watch program in its member neighborhoods. Project Manager: Bethany Davidson

№: 31\100 **Raising Pittsburgh's Black History Awareness through Literature** Awarded: $5,000

United Black Book Clubs of Pittsburgh collaborated with the Allegheny County Library Association to create an intergenerational literacy project surrounding *The WPA History of the Negro in Pittsburgh*, a historical non-fiction work edited by University of Pittsburgh Professor of History Laurence Glasco. Project Manager: Diane Turner

№: **32**\100   **ReTool Local Economies Forum**
Awarded: $5,000

ReTool organized a participatory art and community project that investigated informal, local economies in Pittsburgh—jitney services, do-it-yourself artists, cottage industries, etc. In partnership with The Union Project, the artists interviewed participants to document the effect that these local economies have on various communities. Project Managers: Robin Hewlett and Carolyn Lambert

№: **33**\100   **Sailing in Pittsburgh**   Awarded: $5,000

Point of Pittsburgh Sailing League promoted sailing on Pittsburgh's rivers with the establishment of a permanent sailing program in Pittsburgh in conjunction with the 2008 Three Rivers Regatta. Project Manager: Joe Kirk

№: **34**\100   **Walkers' Festival 2008**   Awarded: $5,000

Walkers' Festival 2008 project increased health and wellness as well as social interaction by identifying and mobilizing participants in new and existing community walking groups. Project Manager: JoAnn Kline

№: **35**\100   **Washington's Encampment**
Awarded: $5,000

Allegheny Foothills Society highlighted the historical events that lead to the founding of Pittsburgh. During Plum Borough's annual community festival in October, the society staged reenactments in Boyce Park, near the site of General John Forbes and Colonel George Washington's encampment on November 22, 1758. Project Manager: Tom Klingensmith
(61)

№: **36**\100   **Women's Voices, Women's Votes: Survey of Women's Issues**   Awarded: $5,000

Executive Women's Council of Greater Pittsburgh brought women's advocacy organizations from throughout Southwestern Pennsylvania together to identify the top issues of importance to women, outlining a strategic agenda to address these issues with public officials, corporations, educational institutions, and foundations. Project Manager: Mary Frances Dean

№: **37**\100   **Youghtoberfest**   Awarded: $5,000

Milestone, Inc. hosted a festival of outdoor recreation opportunities and activities for individuals with disabilities. The event occurred during October at the Youghiogheny River Trail Gardens park between the Youghiogheny River and the Youghiogheny River Bike Trail in Elizabeth Township. Project Manager: Kate Bayer

ARMSTRONG

Projects: 7 \ Total Awarded: $24,300

№: **38**\100   **Allegheny Echoes**   Awarded: $1,000

Armstrong County Public Libraries replicated a program from the Children's Museum of Pittsburgh to Armstrong County. "Pennsylvania History through Folk Music" was an interactive, hands-on workshop about the region's multicultural and historical heritage featuring authentic Appalachian instruments and sing-along activities. Project Manager: Timi Kost

№: **39**\100   **Apollo Memorial Library Centennial: Return to 1908**   Awarded: $1,500

Apollo Memorial Library celebrated the ordinary accomplishments of early American settlers and gave modern day residents, young and old, a rejuvenated sense of civic pride by reacquainting them with the people of the past who built their hometown. Project Manager: Judy Turner

№: **40**\100   **Imagine What You Can See Here**
Awarded: $4,320

Freeport Renaissance Association installed signage along a portion of the Buffalo Creek Rails to Trails path near Freeport highlighting the diversity wildlife that make this area an Important Birding Area according to The Audubon Society. Project Manager: Mary Bowlin

№: **41**\100   **Postage Stamp Park**   Awarded: $5,000

Parker City Revitalization Corporation created the Postage Stamp Park—a small park along the riverfront in the central business district of this "Smallest City in the USA." Project Managers: William and Marilyn McCall
(76)

№: **42**\100   **Roaring Run Natural Area Hiking and Biking Brochure**   Awarded: $2,500

Roaring Run Watershed Association created a hiking and biking brochure to showcase the Roaring Run Trail, the Rock Furnace Trail, hiking and biking trails, canoe and kayak launches, waterways, and scenic vistas near Apollo on the Kiskiminetas River. Project Manager: Rich Dixon

№: **43**\100   Spotlight on the Community
Awarded: $5,000

Downtown Kittanning, Inc. held free public movie screenings in the amphitheatre at The Wilbur Bower Community Park in Kittanning during summer 2008. Project Manager: Marilyn Davidson

№: **44**\100   Sugarcreek Community Days
Awarded: $5,000

Sugarcreek Community Coalition hosted Sugarcreek Community Days, an event to establish a sense of community, promote important ideals, celebrate patriotic pride, and showcase citizens and veterans both past and present in rural Sugarcreek Township. Project Manager: Vincent King

BEAVER

Projects: 8 \ Total Awarded: $40,000

№: **45**\100   Art-Repreneurship   Awarded: $5,000

Center for Creative Arts Expression engaged young artists in Beaver Falls to utilize recycled materials and the resources of second-hand shops to create, display, and market their creativity. The project culminated with the Beaver Falls Unified Arts Festival hosted by Beaver Falls High School. Project Manager: Geraldine McCorr

№: **46**\100   Beaver County River-Town Community Walking Maps   Awarded: $5,000

To promote health and exercise, highlight points of interest, and encourage residents to celebrate the towns' unique treasures, this project designed, published, and distributed walking maps of the many river-towns of Beaver County. Project Manager: Valentine Brkich *(101)*

№: **47**\100   First Company Fort McIntosh Garrison Revitalization   Awarded: $5,000

Beaver Area Heritage Foundation helped to equip the reenactment regiment representing the Fort McIntosh Garrison of 1778 with new uniforms and gunpowder for muskets and cannons. The fort, on the bank of the Ohio River in Beaver, was the first permanent peacetime post of the U.S. Army and is a Beaver County connection to the Revolutionary War. Project Managers: Dick Buckus and Midge Sefton *(61)*

№: **48**\100   Gateway to Ambridge   Awarded: $5,000

Committee to Clean and Beautify Ambridge revitalized the points of entry into Ambridge, a former company town named for the American Bridge Company. The gateways became a source of pride for residents and a symbol of community change. Project Manager: Roberta Sciulli *(71–72)*

№: **49**\100   Monaca 15th Street Playground Shelter   Awarded: $5,000

Monaca Recreation Board enhanced the 15th Street playground in Monaca by constructing an attractive shelter for use as a gathering place by neighborhood residents, visitors, a nearby daycare facility, and a grade school. Project Managers: Theo Polce and Laura Rubino

№: **50**\100   Times Tabloid for Beaver County Historical Organizations   Awarded: $5,000

Beaver County Historical Research and Landmarks Foundation purchased a tabloid promotion in the Beaver County Times with synopses of local historical societies and groups to promote historical sites and organizations in Beaver County. Project Manager: Brenda Applegate

№: **51**\100   A Vietnam Remembrance
Awarded: $5,000

Beaver County Chapter 862 of the Vietnam Veterans of America sponsored a Remembrance Week in the parks of Beaver coinciding with the appearance of a traveling model of the Vietnam Veterans Memorial wall in September 2008. Project Manager: Larry Googins

№: **52**\100   YouthCares Computer Recycling
Awarded: $5,000

Job Training for Beaver County provided disadvantaged youth in Beaver County an opportunity to de-manufacture computers, acquire invaluable job skills, and save computers from polluting the region's landfills. Project Manager: Richard Riley

BEDFORD

Projects: 3 \ Total Awarded: $15,000

№: 53\100 Ft. Bedford Park Riverfront Trail Promenade Awarded: $5,000
Borough of Bedford constructed a trail along the Raystown Branch of the Juniata River, connecting the newly renovated Bedford Springs Hotel to Fort Bedford Park in downtown Bedford and then to Old Bedford Village. Project Manager: John Montgomery

№: 54\100 Old Bedford Village Redoubt and Encampment Awarded: $5,000
Old Bedford Village built fortifications around the encampment that match those found there in 1758, adding to the historical veracity and atmosphere of battle reenactments. Project Manager: Roger Kirwin *(54–55)*

№: 55\100 Schellsburg Community Park Awarded: $5,000
Schellsburg Borough improved Schellsburg Borough Park in time for the borough's bicentennial in 2008. Improvements included a walking trail, horseshoe pits, shrubbery, lighting, bathroom facilities, a monument to the town's founder John Schell, and a veteran's memorial. Project Manager: Dorothy Wolfhope

BUTLER

Projects: 7 \ Total Awarded: $33,800

№: 56\100 Fine Arts and Beyond Showcase Awarded: $5,000
Golden Tornado Scholastic Foundation enhanced, expanded, and promoted a showcase of artistic and musical work from Butler Area School District students and professional artists from the community. Project Manager: Jerry Slamecka

№: 57\100 Gibson Music and Pixel Perfect Teen Programming Awarded: $5,000
Butler County Family YMCA provided Butler teens with programs in music and digital photography to impart new skills, promote self-esteem, build a sense of community, and create outlets for artistic expression. Project Manager: Corinne Coulson

№: 58\100 Jay Bee Model Circus Awarded: $5,000
Butler County Historical Society added the Jay Bee Model Circus—a wooden, hand-carved and -painted, miniature model circus by local artist James Bashline—to its permanent collection. The Society will exhibit, preserve, and maintain this one-of-a-kind model that took over 50 years to complete. Project Manager: Rebecca Crum-Reinsel *(128–129)*

№: 59\100 Petrolia Area Historical Project Awarded: $3,810
Petrolia Area Historical Project detailed the history of Petrolia and its surrounding area, beginning with the first settlers in 1795 and progressing through the oil boom of 1872, the oil bust of 1880, and the events, industries, and people that enabled Petrolia to survive to the present day. Project Manager: Joe McCloskey

№: 60\100 Slippery Rock University Green and Growing Awarded: $5,000
Slippery Rock University Student Government Association offered green bikes as an alternative means of transportation on and around the campus and planted more than 100 trees to sustain the land and create beautiful spaces promoting learning, recreation, and community gathering. Project Managers: Diane Wolak and Steven Roberts *(149–152)*

№: 61\100 Succop Conservancy Hay Wagon Restoration Awarded: $5,000
Succop Conservancy restored a hay wagon housed in a bank barn on its property. The finished hay wagon became a landmark for the Heritage School at The Conservancy, an experiential learning center preserving utilitarian crafts, arts, and trades in Butler. Project Manager: Nancy Lawry *(57)*

№: **62**\100   **Website for Butler Downtown Revitalization**   Awarded: $5,000

Butler Downtown Revitalization Committee stimulated neighborhood and business district revitalization by promoting a sense of place, high quality of life, and the economic vitality of downtown Butler through a website that coordinated efforts and increased its membership. Project Manager: James Hrabrosky

CAMBRIA

Projects: 5 \ Total Awarded: $25,000

№: **63**\100   **Haw's Pike Welcome Garden**   Awarded: $5,000

Morrelville-Oakhurst Revitalization created a more welcoming entrance to Johnstown by landscaping an area at the Route 56-Haw's Pike entrance to the city. Project Manager: Marie Mock

№: **64**\100   **Haynes Street Underpass Sculpture**   Awarded: $5,000

Johnstown Public Art Alliance and City of Johnstown's Department of Community and Economic Development created an attractive parklet featuring a signature, large-scale sculpture by John Stallings, with public seating and decorative plantings in the gateway neighborhood of Kernville. Project Manager: Cindy Stallings *(49)*

№: **65**\100   **Parent and Child Together Play Space**   Awarded: $5,000

Beginnings, Inc. purchased play room equipment and sensory development tools to create an indoor play space to meet the needs of young children developing normally as well as those with disabilities and developmental delays. Project Manager: Cathy Bafia

№: **66**\100   **Planting Connections: Our Cambrian Garden**   Awarded: $5,000

Cambria County Historical Society installed new landscaping at the 1889 A.W. Buck House reflective of the Victorian era in which it was built. Project Manager: Dave Huber *(70–71)*

№: **67**\100   **Sandyvale Memorial Botanical Gardens**   Awarded: $5,000

Sandyvale Cemetery Association rehabilitated and utilized a recently donated building to serve as the initial visitor's area for the Sandyvale Memorial Botanical Garden in Johnstown. Project Managers: William Horner and Diana Kabo *(75)*

FAYETTE

Projects: 5 \ Total Awarded: $24,400

№: **68**\100   **Connellsville Historic Heritage Walking Trail**   Awarded: $5,000

Connellsville Historical Society created a walking trail that informs hikers of the cultural, ethnic, and industrial make up Connellsville. The trail is dotted with signs that tell the tales of Connellsville and feature historical photographs from the Carnegie Library. Project Manager: Michael Edwards *(100)*

№: **69**\100   **Connellsville Trail Town Public Art Project**   Awarded: $5,000

Connellsville Redevelopment Authority seeded community-based public art in Connellsville in conjunction with the Great Allegheny Passage Trail Town Program. The work created a gateway to the community and encouraged trail users to stop and visit the town. Project Manager: Ralph Wombacker

№: **70**\100   **Everson Borough Veterans Parklet**   Awarded: $4,375

Everson Civics Organization established a memorial parklet in Everson to honor those who served and those who continue to serve the country in the Armed Forces. Project Manager: Tim Shoemaker

№: **71**\100   **Main Street Classic 5K Run/Walk for the Homeless**   Awarded: $5,000

City Mission-Living Stones hosted this event in Uniontown to raise support and awareness of the community's homeless neighbors. Project Managers: Dexter Smart and Vicki Yauger *(110)*

№: **72**\100   **Touchstone Pioneer Craft Days**   Awarded: $5,000

Touchstone Center for Crafts enhanced and expanded the Mountain Crafts Festival in rural Farmington to an entire weekend. Activities included studio demonstrations, participatory art projects, fiddling and clogging competitions, and buckwheat cake meals. Project Manager: Scott Hillard

GREENE

Projects: 2 \ Total Awarded: $10,000

№: 73\100 Creative Industries: Second Saturday Seminars Awarded: $5,000
Nathanael Green Historical Foundation expanded its annual conference on the importance of creativity in the community to 10 individually-focused seminars in Greensboro. The sessions explored how art can be socially relevant, educationally significant, and economically viable for rural communities as well as urban areas. Project Manager: Becky David

№: 74\100 ReDiscovering Eden: Historic Waynesburg Walking Tour Awarded: $5,000
Waynesburg Prosperous and Beautiful created illustrative and whimsical tour maps featuring vintage photographs and fun trivia to guide visitors through the town center and college campus in Waynesburg, an area the town's founder termed "Eden."
Project Manager: Mary Beth Pastorius *(100–101)*

INDIANA

Projects: 4 \ Total Awarded: $19,700

№: 74\100 A Day in the Life of an Enslaved Child Awarded: $5,000
Passport to Freedom created an interactive exhibit at the Underground Railroad History Center in Blairsville to educate schoolchildren about the typical daily activities of an enslaved child of African origin in the United States during the 1800s.
Project Manager: Denise Jennings-Doyle

№: 75\100 Indiana County Covered Bridge Festival Awarded: $5,000
Indiana County Parks and Trails celebrated the four covered bridges of Indiana County during an all-day festival in Blue Spruce Park in September 2008. The event featured tours led by covered bridge enthusiasts and showcased local artisans and crafters demonstrating their work.
Project Manager: Ed Patterson

№: 76\100 Tanoma Abandoned Mine Drainage Wetlands Educational Trail Awarded: $4,680
Evergreen Conservancy added informational signs to a nature trail in the recently-acquired Tanoma Wetlands, a 10-acre abandoned coal mine drainage passive treatment system. The signs included information about the methods used to revitalize the previously-polluted water supply. Project Manager: Cindy Rogers *(99)*

№: 77\100 W.R. McIlwain Store and Warehouse Preservation Project Awarded: $5,000
Saltsburg Borough preserved the historic W.R. McIlwain Store and Warehouse. Known locally as "The Mule Barn," the 157-year old structure was transformed from a dilapidated eyesore into a restored historic site. Project Managers: PJ Hruska and Jack Maguire *(55–57)*

LAWRENCE

Projects: 2 \ Total   Awarded: $7,000

№: 78\100 American Red Cross Kids Club Awarded: $2,000
Lawrence County American Red Cross encouraged children of all ages to learn life-saving disaster preparedness skills and volunteer their time and help people through the Red Cross Kids Club program.
Project Manager: John Stubbs

№: 79\100 Lockley Kindergarten Center Playground Awarded: $5,000
New Castle Area School District contributed to the construction of an outdoor play space for children attending Lockley Kindergarten and provide for its ongoing maintenance. Project Manager: Deb DeBlasio

MERCER

Projects: 6 \ Total Awarded: $27,400

№: 80\100 C3 Performance Car Care Ministry Awarded: $5,000
Central Community Church established an innovative new ministry service offering routine vehicle maintenance and educational classes to low-income families in Transfer, a rural community with no access to public transportation. Project Manager: Pastor Phillip Beck *(106–107)*

№: 81\100 Grandma's Good Eats! Awarded: $2,564
Girl Scouts of Penn Lakes Council created an intergenerational cooking program connecting Girl Scouts and their grandparents in Farrell. Working together, the participants learned not only how to cook classic family recipes, but how to make them healthier. Project Manager: Anita Schrott

№: 82\100 GRASP Tutoring Awarded: $5,000
Greenville Regional After School Program (GRASP) expanded its service in the school districts of Mercer County offering positive after school options to promote healthy choices, strong friendships, academic support, and spiritual involvement. Project Manager: Ronald Vennare

№: 83\100 Grove City College Student Philanthropy Project Awarded: $5,000
Grove City College established a partnership between faculty, students, philanthropists, and the surrounding communities to introduce students to the challenges of fundraising and grantmaking. Students determined objectives for their community investments, the method for identifying and communicating with potential recipients, and the criteria used to make small grants. Project Manger: Brian Powell *(149)*

№: 84\100 Telepsychiatry Program Awarded: $5,000
Community Counseling Center of Mercer County addressed the ongoing shortage of local psychiatric assistance by using technology to connect rural residents to the specialized expertise of psychiatrists at the Western Psychiatric Institute and Clinic in Pittsburgh. Project Manager: Fern Torok

№: 85\100 Youth Advocate Project Awarded: $5,000
AWARE piloted a unique blend of risk-reducing education and victim support services directed at students who attend Grove City area schools. The program developed skills and strategies that young people can employ to reduce the negative impact of violence in their lives. Project Manager: Lizette Olsen *(152–153)*

SOMERSET

Projects: 4 \ Total Awarded: $20,000

№: 86\100 Arcadia Theater's 10th Anniversary Celebration Awarded: $5,000
Arcadia Theater hosted its 10th anniversary celebration and established an endowment for the theater, which opened in 1912 to host vaudeville and later cinema productions. Damaged by the floods of 1977, the theater reopened in 1998 as a regional performing arts venue in Windber. Project Manager: Denise Mihalick *(58)*

№: 87\100 Ferrellton Community Sports Park Concession Stand Awarded: $5,000
Jenner Township Community Park Fund helped to erect a concession stand with restrooms at the Ferrellton Community Sports Park in Jenner Township. Project Manager: Keith Barnick

№: 88\100 Interfaith Spiritual Healing Meditation Awarded: $5,000
Institute of Integrative Medicine at Windber Medical Center created a guided labyrinth walkway and built a sustainable health care system that integrated mind, body, and spirit through interfaith spiritual healing meditation. Project Managers: Jean Brinker and Rachel Allen

№: 89\100 Meyersdale Tennis Courts Renovation Awarded: $5,000
Meyersdale Area School District funded renovations to three of its tennis courts as a capstone project to its capital improvement campaign. Project Manager: Tracey Karlie

WASHINGTON

Projects: 2 \ Total Awarded: $10,000

№: 90\100 Bradford's Kitchen Reconstruction
Awarded: $5,000
Bradford House Historical Association restored aspects of the historic 18th-century home of David Bradford who would become, along with his extravagant house, a central figure in the Whiskey Rebellion of 1794. Project Manager: Clay Kilgore

№: 91\100 It Takes You: Campaign to End Poverty in our Community Awarded: $5,000
Community Action Southwest contributed to an outreach campaign to increase the awareness of poverty and foster increased volunteer efforts to combat poverty and hunger in Washington County. Project Manager: Connie Ferris

WESTMORELAND

Projects: 9 \ Total Awarded: $42,000

№: 92\100 Community Supported Agriculture Facility Upgrade Awarded: $4,800
Sarver's Hill Farms built a new, green-as-possible barn to better serve its Community Supported Agriculture Program and provide a place to hold educational agriculture and nutrition programming for the community. Project Manager: Paul Sarver

№: 93\100 Compass Inn Museum Living History
Awarded: $5,000
Ligonier Valley Historical Society promoted history education and appreciation through living history events that helped raise awareness of the Compass Inn Museum—a unique, underused historical attraction in Laughlintown. Project Manager: Jim Koontz

№: 94\100 Downtown Greensburg Asset Image Campaign Awarded: $2,400
Greensburg Community Development Corporation purchased vinyl street light pole banners to line the historic and cultural districts of Greensburg and enhance the aesthetic nature of this heavily traveled commercial district. Project Manager: Steven Gifford

№: 95\100 JAYS After School Program
Awarded: $5,000
Communities In Schools supported the Joining to Achieve Youth Success (JAYS) Program, a grassroots, community-based, voluntary after school academic enrichment program offered at no cost to students attending McKee Middle School in Jeanette.
Project Manager: Don Bartowick

№: 96\100 Operation Fresh Express Awarded: $5,000
Westmoreland County Food Bank expanded Operation Fresh Express—a program to distribute perishable food items throughout Westmoreland County—by providing increased distributions in Greensburg, Monessen, and Mount Pleasant.
Project Manager: Deana Pastor *(108)*

№: 97\100 Pay It Forward Initiative Awarded: $5,000
Schooner Youth Center, Inc. funded its Pay it Forward Initiative in Monessen, a program that empowered youth, with the assistance of community mentors, to design and implement three community-based projects. Project Manager: Jennifer Melnick Carota

№: 98\100 Pioneer Point Public Arts Heritage Project Awarded: $5,000
Downtown West Newton, Inc. seeded the creation of community-based public art in West Newton in conjunction with the Great Allegheny Passage Trail Town Program. The artwork commemorated the historic trek of the Northwest Territory Expedition.
Project Manager: Benjamin Markle

№: 99\100 Westmoreland County History Education Program Awarded: $5,000
Westmoreland Heritage and the Westmoreland County Historical Society established a speakers bureau to provide free living historians and knowledgeable speakers to schools, historical groups, and other organizations across Westmoreland County.
Project Manager: Tom Headley *(143)*

№: 100\100 Westmoreland Earth Day 2008—Greening Your Footprint Awarded: $5,000
St. Vincent College collaborated with more than 60 regional organizations to address issues of environmental stewardship on Earth Day 2008.
Project Manager: Angela Belli

COMMUNITY CONNECTIONS COMMITTEE

Gregg Behr
Karen Blumen
Charles Burke, Jr.
JoAnne Burley
Bracken Burns, Sr.
John Cardone
Frank Clark
Debbie Corll
Bob DeWitt
Judie Donaldson
Colleen Fedor
Sylvia Fields
Laura Fisher
Schuyler Foerster
Evan Frazier
Jay Gilmer
Kimberly Hammer
Susan Hockenberry
Donna Holdorf

David Kahley
Colleen Kalchthaler
Ellen Kight
Eric Mann
Teresa Stoughton Marafino
Marguerite Jarrett Marks
Bruce McDowell
Sally Mizerak
Muriel Nuttall
Don Orlando
Martha Riecks
Katherine Risko
Grace Robinson
Norma Ryan
William Thompkins
Elisa Vettier
Stephanie Williams
Constance Yarris
Mary Zacherl
Peter Zerega
Blair Zimmerman

Co-Chairs
Aradhna Dhanda (left)
George Miles Jr.
Cathy Lewis Long

DECISIONMAKING PANELISTS

Regional

Ron Aldom
Lena Andrews
Diana Bucco
Janis Burley-Wilson
Bracken Burns, Sr.
Chuck Burtyk
Steve Catt
Sarah Coon
John Dawes
James Denova
Sharon Dilworth
Dennis Gilfoyle
Larry Haynes
Donna Holdorf
Mike Kane
Dusty Kirk
Patricia Kirkpatrick
Daniel Lavelle
Paul Leger
Robbie Matesic
JoAnn McBride
Mary Jo Morandini
Ann Nemanic
Leslie Orbin
Clara Pascoe
Lindsay Patross
Rick Pierchalski
Minette Seate
Kimberly Walkenhorst
Ryan Walsh
Abby Wilson

Allegheny County

Shannon Anglero
Betty Arenth
Martin Ashby
Susan Blackman
Diasmer Bloe
Bill Bodine
Kate Bowers
David Conrad
Veronica Corpuz
Tom Croft
Greg Crowley
Joanna Deming
John Denny
Sarah Dieleman-Perry
Mike Edwards
Sean Fabich
Mary Fisher
Court Gould
Sally Haas
Ben Harrison
Angie Kazmeraski
Cynthia Maleski
Erin Molchany
Sara Radelet
Arlene Sparks
Jaylin Thomas
Will Thompkins
Sid Wiesner
Laura Zinski

Armstrong County

Randy Cloak
Mindy Knappenberger
Connie Mateer
Sondra Mervis
Jeffrey Pyle
James Seagriff, Jr.
Virginia Steimer
Autumn Vorpe-Seyler

Beaver County

Jennifer Buchanan Rapach
Kristen Denne
Claire Grotevant
Jack Manning
Jim Marshall
Victoria Michaels
Tom Patterson
Robert Rice
Laura Rubino
Terry Turkovich

Bedford County

Lynn Ashe
Daniel Burns
William Defibaugh
Edward Garlock
Dick Hess
Kay Reynolds
Leslie Rock

Butler County

Jack Cohen
Larry Garvin
John Haven
Jeff Kelley
Sheryl Kelly
Kathy Kline
Rebekah Sheeler
David Todd
Elan Welter-Lewis

Cambria County
Karen Azer
Erik Foley
Jeanne Gleason
Bruce Haselrig
Susan Mann
Rob McCombie
Kenneth Salem
Renee Shaw
Leah Spangler
Robin Strachan

Fayette County
Valerie Bacharach
Donald Bartowick
Jeremy Burnworth
Deberah Kula
Susan McCarthy
Muriel Nuttall
Clara Pascoe
Sue Quinn
Marty Schiff

Greene County
Shelly Brown
William DeWeese
Karen Galentine
Janice Hatfield

Tara Kinsell
Norma Kline
James O'Connell
Linda Rush
Mary Shine
Bettie Stammerjohn

Indiana County
Ken Bisbee
Chris Catalfamo
Leann Chaney
Andrew Davis
Kate Geiger
Marti Higgins
Denise Jennings-Doyle
Shirley Johnson
Rita Nichols
Dave Reed

Lawrence County
Deb DeBlasio
Betty Ann DiMuccio
Tom Ford
Robert Hardy

Kim Koller-Jones
Mike Lysakowski
Robert McCracken
Jackie Meade
Kim Rogers

Mercer County
Erik Bielata
Larry Haynes
Mark Longietti
Lynda Moss-McDougall
Leann Smith
Ann Marie Spiardi
Angelo Stamoolis
Michael Wright

Somerset County
Grant Atwell
Michele Beener
Kerri Burtner
Curtis Kerns
Michael Knecht
Vicki Meier
Denise Mihalick
Gloria Pritts
Rae Ann Weaver
Stephanie Williams

Washington County
Mark Alterici
Christine Blaine
Rick Burke
Jay Dutton
Lucy Northrop
William Price
Kathy Sabol
William Speakman
Betsie Trew

Westmoreland County
Glenn Cavanaugh
Christine Foschia
Alexander Graziani
Tom Headley
Gene James
Patricia Kowatch
Cathy McCollom
Kate Patton
Brent Scholar

About the Author

As the documentarian of Community Connections, I had the pleasure of spending 2008 meeting the people who made Pittsburgh 250 remarkable, from Bedford to Mercer and back again. But in trying to get in touch with the region, I discovered much more: An opportunity to fuel up on the high-octane black 'n' gold manna that is the people, places, and stories of Pittsburgh.

Some of those stories appear in this volume; so many more, of course, do not. But all of them attest to the eccentric beauty of the region we share as our home. Over the past year, it feels as though I've learned more than in the previous dozen: About Southwestern Pennsylvania, sure, but more so about the catalytic energy and indomitable spirit that arises when ordinary people are given the opportunity to show that they're hardly ordinary at all.

JUSTIN HOPPER, February, 2009

For more than ten years, Justin Hopper has covered Pittsburgh's art, music, history and culture as a writer for a broad variety of publications. After four years as a writer and section editor for Pittsburgh *City Paper*, he left to pursue a freelance career. Hopper's work has appeared in regional publications including *Pittsburgh*, *Carnegie* and *Pitt* magazines and *Pop City* online journal, where his "Gospel of Pittsburgh" proved one of the site's most popular essays.

Nationally, Hopper has written about music, art, travel and culture writing for publications such as *Paste*, *XLR8R*, *Spin*, as well as other magazines and web sites, often concerning either Pittsburgh or his other primary interest: obscure English culture and history. He is currently working on two book projects: an exploration of England's 100-mile South Downs Way, and a history of popular music during the British miner's strike of 1984–85.

About The Sprout Fund

The Sprout Fund enriches the Pittsburgh region's vitality by engaging citizens, amplifying voices, supporting creativity and innovation, and cultivating connected communities.

Founded in 2001, Sprout facilitates community-led solutions to regional challenges and supports efforts to create a thriving, progressive, and culturally diverse region. With strong working relationships to many community organizations and regional stakeholders, The Sprout Fund is one of Southwestern Pennsylvania's leading agencies on issues related to civic engagement, talent attraction and retention, public art, and catalytic small-scale funding.

Sprout Seed Awards are modest financial awards that support community-based projects and strategic initiatives. Sprout Public Art enhances the visual landscape of neighborhoods and communities by creating high-quality public art in a collaborative community process with local artists. Engage Pittsburgh promoted civic engagement and supported projects of community interest through ideation and online discussion. Community Connections was a grassroots initiative of Pittsburgh 250 supporting projects that encouraged civic engagement to commemorate the region's 250th anniversary. Spark energizes the creativity of children in Southwestern Pennsylvania through support for technology and new media projects. Hothouse, the summer's hottest party, is Sprout's "live annual report" to the community and a major fundraising event.

Sprout is dedicated to serving those who demonstrate the drive and capacity to think creatively about their communities. Directed by a board of young, creative, and civically engaged people and led by co-founders Cathy Lewis Long and Matt Hannigan, Sprout is located in the Penn Avenue Arts District in the East End of Pittsburgh. Supported by lead contributions from the Richard King Mellon Foundation, Sprout has also received funding from more than 20 local foundations and more than 65 corporations, nonprofits, and governmental entities.

With ongoing local support and continued appreciation by the communities it serves, The Sprout Fund will continue to catalyze creative solutions to pressing challenges, engage people in community conversations, respond to the needs of its target audiences, open doors to civic participation, and promote responsible stewardship of community interests.

With Thanks

The co-chairs of Pittsburgh 250 Community Connections, Aradhna Dhanda, Cathy Lewis Long, and George Miles, Jr., would like to offer thanks the following organizations and individuals for their dedicated support of Pittsburgh 250 Community Connections and *Making the Connections*. To the members of the Community Connections Committee, who envisioned that a grassroots funding program could touch every corner of our region—you made this a priority, thereby speeding its development and enabling its growth. To Bill Flanagan, Pam Golden, and the rest of the staff at the Allegheny Conference on Community Development for their interminable work throughout Pittsburgh's 250th anniversary year. To the project managers, for working with such diligence and devotion. To the moderators and facilitators, for traveling to every county in Southwestern Pennsylvania armed with a brush and a pen, ready to help determine what "Our Community Is…" To the expert reviewers and decisionmakers, for thoughtfully participating in a process that was designed to give you the power to choose what was best for our communities at this unique moment in time. To the private foundations, who in many ways provided the spark that set this program aflame: Your support and guidance, in the early stages, was critical to the eventual success of the program. A special thank you to the members of the funding community who took an early and active role in supporting Community Connections: Pat Getty, Scott Izzo, and Gregg Behr—thank you for your leadership and commitment to this initiative. To the corporate community, for your support and commitment to the betterment of our region: It is no secret that the generosity of companies across Southwestern Pennsylvania contributes largely to the quality of life we enjoy here. To the community foundations who proved to be invaluable partners: Gaining your financial support was key, but building upon your networks of influence was, perhaps, even more important to establishing a truly regional initiative. To our media partners, Pittsburgh *Post-Gazette*, WDUQ-FM, and deepLocal, who created both opportunities for promotion and innovative tools to promote this program. To the board and staff of The Sprout Fund, for your continued guidance and support; in particular, the tireless work of Dustin Stiver, Matt Hannigan, and Ryan Coon does not go unnoticed. To Jennifer McNulty for keeping the monthly Community Connections newsletter looking fresh. To our photographers Nathan Schritter and Nate Boguszewski for capturing so many faces and memorable sites of Southwestern Pennsylvania. To Justin Hopper, the voice of Community Connections, whose insightful reportage, epic prosody, and unending wit captured its stories perfectly. And also to Landesberg Design, for their keen eye and instructive advice. This program's success is indebted to all of these contributors and others still, for their commitment to this important regional initiative.

The Sprout Fund Board of Directors

Laurel Brandstetter
Mark Broadhurst
Edgar Um Bucholtz
David Caliguiri
Lou Castelli
Danielle Crumrine
Pete Eberhart
Elvira Eichleay
Jasdeep Khaira
Cathy Lewis Long
Christian Manders
Anne Sekula
Henry J. Simonds

The Sprout Fund Staff

Cathy Lewis Long
Matt Hannigan
Timothy Blevins
Ryan Coon
Curt Gettman
Mac Howison
Dustin Stiver

Pittsburgh 250, Inc. Staff

Bill Flanagan
Laura Fisher
Pamela Golden
Robert Petrilli

An initiative of the Allegheny Conference on Community Development

James E. Rohr, *Chair*
F. Michael Langley, *CEO*

The Sprout Fund \ 5423 Penn Avenue, Pittsburgh, PA 15206-3423 \ 412.325.0646 \ sproutfund.org